To Hell and Back:
My Life as an Abused Husband

To Hell and Back:
My Life as an Abused Husband

Kimber Broughton

iUniverse, Inc.
Bloomington

To Hell and Back: My Life as an Abused Husband

iUniverse books may be ordered through booksellers or by contacting:

iUniverse
1663 Liberty Drive
Bloomington, IN 47403
www.iuniverse.com
1-800-Authors (1-800-288-4677)

ISBN: 978-1-4759-0629-5 (sc)
ISBN: 978-1-4759-0631-8 (hc)
ISBN: 978-1-4759-0630-1 (ebk)

Printed in the United States of America

iUniverse rev. date: 04/24/2012

Contents

Preface

Memories . . .

Why do we only remember certain things? Why don't we remember everything? Is that even possible?

The human brain is a very complicated organ, with neurons and synapses engaged in endless activity as we struggle not only to process the things occurring around us, but also to understand our own thoughts. So why does an event we haven't thought of for 25 years sometimes bob to the surface?

Let's consider a computer. When we delete information, where does it go? I remember someone once saying, jokingly, that the data traveled down the electrical lines backwards and disappeared into the wall socket, into oblivion. We all know this isn't true. A good computer analyst can bring deleted files back. However, can this be done with the human brain? No one really knows for sure.

There are times, however, when we purposely shield ourselves from memories, when we actually block them from our conscious awareness. The brain can be said to have an alarm system in place to protect us—a very complex defense mechanism for our own safety.

When I first met my husband, he seemed to be as normal as the next guy. He did tell me that he was coming out of a very bad marriage, and we often talked about his experiences. We eventually wed, and things were smooth sailing for a couple years or so. Then all hell broke loose. As one doctor told me, our minds have been known to wait until we are happy and healthy before blocked memories rear their ugly heads. He also said it's usually at the happiest times of our lives when those memories sneak to the surface.

The brain is trying to "cleanse" itself in such times, he said.

That's exactly what happened to my husband: the dam broke when he was driving home from work one afternoon. According to the police, he was found in a catatonic state, driving erratically and unaware of his surroundings. The next day, he awoke in the hospital with absolutely no recall of the previous day's events. But for two years afterward, he could not work, drive, or function at full capacity.

Over the years, as he would relate the horrors of his previous marriage, I kept a journal. Eventually I revealed my writings to him—and he wholeheartedly approved when I suggested that we publish them, in an attempt to help other men who have endured (or are enduring) experiences such as his. My husband, always trying to find humor in life, came up with the chapter titles.

I may have written and published it, but this is an "as told to" story; it's very much my husband's tale.

1
Introduction

Call me Jonathan, though that's not my real name. Because the events I'll discuss in this book actually occurred, names have been changed to protect the innocent and, yes, the guilty too. In the pages that follow, I'll discuss a bitter reality that many men experience but are conditioned by our society to hide: domestic abuse at the hands of a spouse.

Much has been written about the opposite scenario—the abuse of women by men. This is a very real and widespread problem, and I have nothing but sympathy for the victims. But the abuse of men at the hands of their women is something that *does* occur, daily, and there are very few (if any) books on the subject. It's less common than the opposite problem; sadly, there's no doubting that. But even when it does occur, it remains in the shadows for various reasons, mostly because of male pride and cultural conditioning. This book is intended to help those men who are living through the nightmare of abuse, to show them how to recognize the warning signs and how to fight free of them, and to help them realize that there's a life beyond an abusive relationship. You can rebuild your pride and find love, real love, again.

Now, I'll be the first to admit that I'm no Phil McGraw or Joyce Brothers; I don't even have a bachelor's degree in psychology, much less any experience at all as a therapist or marriage counselor. So what qualifies me as an expert? My own personal experience: I lived it. From 1993-2005, I worked my way through the graduate school of a hellish marriage, one that still haunts me psychologically today.

2

The Beginning of the End

For more than ten years of my life, I was married to a she-devil. There's no better way to put it.

It didn't start out that way, of course, but within six months of marrying my dream girl, my life had devolved into a hell on earth, a morass of abuse, psychological torture, and financial rape. I often looked around at other people and wondered, "What am I doing wrong? Why can't we be like that couple? They look so in love, so happy! Is it me? Am I being punished? *Why?*"

One of my good friends, a co-worker, had told me that he and his wife never argued. He said they had disagreements, but when they did, they'd stay away from each other for an hour or so, and then act as if nothing had happened. I'd always heard the term "agree to disagree," but couldn't envision it happening in my marriage.

I'd decided, by then, that I must have had bad taste when it came to picking women. I'd always been shy and quiet; maybe I just took the first thing that came along. Maybe I'd lowered my standards too far, settling for less than I should have after my disappointing first marriage. I didn't have an outgoing "Type A" personality; I preferred to be the man behind the curtain. Almost all of my dates had been with women I'd been introduced to or set up with on blind dates. That's how I met my first wife, Carrie.

When Carrie told me she wanted a divorce after seven years of marital bliss, I was taken completely by surprise. I knew we'd grown in different directions over the years, but I hadn't realized things had gotten so bad. I've never been one to handle rejection well, and the idea of a divorce tore me apart. I reluctantly left and went to live with my parents while we hammered out the details of a separation agreement. I didn't do well. At the urging of family, I began seeing a counselor to deal with the pain and humiliation. I felt I was a failure to myself and my child. It was the roughest time of my life—or so I thought at the time.

Divorce and depression tend to be synonymous, especially when the divorce comes as a surprise. It can be traumatic to reminisce about the day your beautiful bride walked down the aisle to join you at the altar. I remember thinking, "Our love will last forever," yet suddenly here she was, telling me she wanted out. Why was she doing this? I hadn't been unfaithful; I hadn't been abusive. We just grew apart. What would my friends and family say? I couldn't face our mutual friends any longer; I didn't know whose side they'd take.

I felt I'd never be happy again. Loneliness became my best friend. I didn't want to go out with family or friends, only to see happy couples together; the memories would flood my mind, intensifying the feelings of despondence and worthlessness. I lost interest in the things I'd previously enjoyed. I didn't sleep well, and found it difficult to concentrate and perform my job. Simple things like getting out of bed, showering, and dressing seemed like too much trouble. It's so much easier to lie in bed and feel sorry for yourself.

My health began to spiral downward. Some people eat their way through a state of depression, only to gain weight and increase their feelings of unattractiveness. I, personally, wouldn't eat; it wasn't worth the effort. I'd go days without eating a good meal, and my reward for punishing myself was severe headaches. On the other hand, there are a select few who can submerge themselves in a rigorous exercise program to release their pent-up frustrations and anger. I joined an exercise club and gave it a good try for two or three weeks, but my heart wasn't in it, and I quit.

My finances were suffering; I was making mortgage and utility payments for a house I wasn't living in. I assumed 75% of our joint expenses, in addition to both child and spousal support. Luckily, I had understanding parents with whom I was able to live rent-free.

I'll always remember the advice I heard over and over again: "Time heals all wounds," and my all-time favorite, "the wheels turn slowly, but they do turn!" I'd also always heard it was the squeaky wheel that got the grease—so I made a lot of noise during the divorce, which only cost me more money in legal fees. I had to listen to unending banter from others who criticized my wife's actions, which only made me defend the woman who'd put me in this situation. A close relative finally demanded of all the critics, "Stop talking about her. The more you talk, the more he'll defend her! Leave him alone, and he'll eventually see things for himself!" That advice proved beneficial. I *did* soon start seeing things in a different light.

The official cause of our divorce was "irreconcilable differences." I was allowed visitation with my six-year-old son every other weekend. I found it difficult to spend quality time with him when I knew that his mother, the woman I still loved, might be out with another man at that very moment.

My friends and coworkers rallied to my side and encouraged me to get involved in activities outside of work. I joined a bowling league, which was enjoyable; I began going to friends' houses on my off days and on the weekends I didn't have my son, and we'd play guitar and have fun together. I was slowly beginning to heal. I even started thinking about female companionship again, yet my shyness remained a constant impediment to finding someone. I was still seeing a psychiatrist and therapist weekly, which gave me the opportunity to talk about it, at least. Was I doing an injustice to my son? Would he think I was trying to replace his mom?

Personal ads had just started appearing in our local newspapers, and I broached the subject with my psychiatrist. I told him I was of the opinion that the women in the ads were loaded with excess emotional baggage and other problems. The doctor replied that I might be surprised; he suggested that there was always the possibility that many of the women were just like me—ladies who were shy, who didn't know how to walk up to a stranger and start a conversation. His advice: give it a try. He gave me his usual speech about meeting in a public place and not revealing too much about myself, pointing out that if I met the person and wasn't impressed or felt threatened, I always had the opportunity to say so and walk away. At his urging, I answered a few ads, and actually met a woman in a very similar situation—her husband had recently left her for another woman. We went out a few times, but the chemistry just wasn't there between us.

My sister had lost her husband a few years earlier in an automobile accident, but she had recovered, and her wisdom and experience were a tremendous help. She'd say, "I know it doesn't look like it now, but things will get better!" She was right. I didn't think I'd ever recover, but the old adage was true: time does heal all wounds.

It was ten months before I began seriously seeing another woman I'd been introduced to by my sister. It was ironic; she'd recently divorced my high school history teacher, something that proved to be very awkward when we went to watch her son play Little League football. We went out a few times, and I thought we were doing okay until, one afternoon, she asked me to take her to a park with a three-mile walking trail. As we talked, she proceeded to tell me that we should just remain friends and not try to advance our relationship to the next level. I learned I'd ruined our chances; it seems I spent a lot of the time we were together talking about my soon-to-be ex and relaying how hurt I was. I hadn't fully recovered.

I went back to spending most of my free time with my friends, playing guitar, and drinking to mask the pain. When my divorce became finalized, I actually felt a wave of relief: it was finally over, and I wasn't hurting anymore.

At first I was reluctant, but eventually I began seeing a woman at work who had a reputation for sexual prowess. She was my exact opposite. She loved the spotlight, and thrived on the attention she received from other men when we'd walk into a nightclub. I'd spend most of my time on a barstool nursing beers while she danced with any willing male in the place. She'd always say, "It doesn't matter who I dance with; I'm going home with you!" After a month of her never-ending sexual energy, I began to wish she *would* go home with someone else. I told her it was beginning to be a job, not an adventure anymore. Naturally, she didn't appreciate that much.

Another woman at work had grown tired of listening to the nymphomaniac's tales of our sex life, which she broadcast to everyone in the cafeteria who'd listen. She approached me and said she had a friend she'd love for me to meet. "You deserve better! She's using you as a play-toy, and you're a nice guy; I don't want to see you get hurt again."

That's how the nightmare began. That was how I met Stacy.

Until then, I'd thought my divorce was the worst experience I would ever endure. But it didn't even come close to what would transpire over the next 12 years of my life.

3

"Come into my Parlor . . ."

I first met Stacy on a weeknight. Taking heed of my doctor's advice, we agreed to meet at a fast food establishment. My first impression was that she was attractive, polite, and courteous. She had three children, two of whom lived with her. She told me that she was currently on a week's vacation from her job as a nurse at a nearby hospital. I'd just met her, and had absolutely no reason to doubt what she said.

We talked for over an hour about various subjects. I learned that her previous husband had died at an early age; he'd suffered a massive heart attack. I clearly saw the pain in her hazel-blue eyes as she recalled the memories of his death. She'd just broken up with her boyfriend—a man who, ironically, I happened to know. His younger brother and I were friends in our teens, and my parents and his had been good friends for over twenty years. It's a small world after all, as the song says.

When it was time to leave, we agreed to see each other again, and made plans for that upcoming Friday night. I suggested dinner, and possibly we'd take in a movie. I left that night with an excited feeling; things appeared to be looking up for me.

That week, I anxiously looked ahead to Friday night, when I'd be able to see Stacy again. When the time came, I spent a considerable amount of time making sure I was dressed nicely before leaving for her house. I arrived at the pre-determined time for our dinner date, and was duly introduced to her son and daughter. Her son and mine happened to be the same age, which was a big plus in both our favors; our boys could play together on the weekends I had visitation with my son.

We enjoyed a nice dinner together and decided to forego the movie and head back to her place to relax and continue our conversation. The time went rapidly; we ended up talking until the wee hours of the morning. On the drive home, I played the night over in my head, and concluded that date had been a terrific success. I'd already decided I definitely wanted to see Stacy again. Much to my delight, she called early the next morning and asked if I'd be interested in getting together to take a leisurely walk at a nearby park. I was more than happy to comply; I'd thoroughly enjoyed her companionship the night before. We ended up spending the entire day together, talking and laughing and enjoying each others' company. I did notice that there were moments when Stacy appeared to be lost in her own thoughts; she appeared to be tuned in to her past. I didn't feel it was my business to pry; possibly she and her deceased husband had also spent time walking together, and the memories had flooded her conscious mind and made her feel sad.

After another dinner together, we went to my parents' home for an informal meet-and-greet. They appeared to be both pleased and impressed with Stacy; she turned on the charm and said exactly the right things. As we were leaving to return to her house, she made a peculiar statement: she promised to take good care of me. I thought surely she was referring to my recent divorce and the hurt I'd suffered.

That Sunday morning we attended church services together. During the service, I noticed that she'd retreated into deep thought again. *Something's lurking beneath the surface,* I remember thinking; but again, I felt it wasn't my business to ask about it. If she wanted to reveal what was troubling her, then I'd find out when she was ready to talk about it. However, I couldn't dismiss the feeling that she was hiding something.

After church, I was taken to meet her parents. They were both very nice and cordial. To hear Stacy telling her parents about me, I was the best thing since sliced bread. Her Mom graciously volunteered to watch the kids, mine included, anytime we wanted to go out and be alone. Stacy had already told them of my shift work and the awkward days off between shifts.

The next morning, Monday, I was off from work. I'd just gotten out of bed when my Mom came upstairs to my bedroom and said she needed to discuss something with me. She'd just received a phone call from a friend, asking her to please accept what she said at face value and advising her to get me away from Stacy—she was bad news! The friend who'd made the call was one of my Mom's oldest friends—the Mother of Stacy's ex-boyfriend. She told my Mom that Stacy never went to work, had lost numerous jobs, and had taken advantage of her son's good-hearted nature by maxing out his credit cards. According to Mom, by the end of the conversation the list of atrocious things Stacy had done was rather extensive.

I wondered then if that might explain those times when Stacy seemed to be lost in thought. I began to have second thoughts; should I take the woman's advice, or should I judge for myself? I realized that when a romance goes sour, things have a tendency to be blown out of proportion, especially to the mother of an affected child; the child's age isn't necessarily relevant. Was she just harboring ill feelings towards Stacy for that reason? I wondered . . . but I have to admit that I had serious doubts about Stacy at this point. The ex-boyfriend's parents had always been nice, Christian people and good friends to my family and me; as mentioned earlier, I grew up with their youngest son. I'd spent many sleepovers at their home over the years, and I'd gone on numerous trips with their family during my teens.

I'd assumed Stacy was working; her vacation had supposedly ended the day before, and I was caught off guard when my phone rang. It was Stacy calling to wish me a good morning, and to invite me over for lunch.

"I thought you were at work," I said slowly.

"Nope, I called and took a vacation day."

"Oh, I see."

I'll say one thing—the woman's damned perceptive. Her next words were, "What's wrong, Jonathan?"

"Well . . . it's probably just a case of sour grapes, so I guess I owe it to you to hear your side of the story."

"What story?" I could sense a stirring of concern in her voice; something was about to happen.

"Your ex's Mom called and talked to my Mom this morning."

"Oh my God! I was afraid this would happen when you told me your family was friends with his. What did she tell your Mom?" Stacy seemed almost frantic.

"She said you never went to work, and maxed out his credit cards and lots of other stuff. What's going on? What happened between the two of you, Stacy?"

"Oh, she's just upset because I broke things off with her son!"

Well, that sounded logical to me; I'd already considered the possibility. I decided to write it off as a scorned mother protecting her son. We agreed on a time for lunch and ended the phone call.

Fifteen minutes later, my phone rang again; it was Stacy on the phone, with a co-worker on three-way calling. She'd called so the co-worker could verify that Stacy did indeed have a job and was taking a vacation day.

That seemed a little strange, but hell, she'd gotten someone to confirm that she was actually employed. Later, when we met for lunch, I looked in her eyes, took her hand, and said, "Stacy, I want to ask you a question."

"Okay."

"I couldn't help but notice last Saturday, while we were walking in the park that at times you appeared to be in your own little world. I noticed it again yesterday in church. Was the thing with your ex's Mom the reason why?"

She looked *so* relieved. "Yes, it was! When you said your family knew his, I thought this could happen, and I don't want your parents to automatically judge me based on what your Mom was told."

I nodded, but I still had my reservations. Stacy knew I was concerned; something didn't add up, and I asked a lot of questions that day. She'd already anticipated my actions; she always seemed to be one step ahead of me. When things got a little deep, she said hurriedly, "Look, my mom said she'll watch the kid's tomorrow night if you'd like to go out of town together. I think some time away would be nice; I know it would do me a lot of good."

Her suggestion couldn't have come at a better time. At work we'd just voted that very day on labor contract negotiations and the majority had voted to go out on strike. I had plenty of free time on my hands now, whether I wanted it or not. "That sounds like fun. Let's plan on doing that."

"Great; I'll call my Mom and let her know. She said she'd give me money to help with the cost; she saw on the news that the plant you work at went on strike. She's so happy I've met someone who's genuinely nice and good-hearted."

Her use of the term "good-hearted" set off alarms. Hadn't they been the exact words her ex's Mom had used? But I stifled my worries and went with it.

The next day, off we went to a popular tourist attraction about an hour away. We stayed overnight, and enjoyed our first sexual encounter. Overall, we had a great time—until the next day, on the way home, when I noticed that faraway look in her eyes again. Soon she started to cry, and I asked why. "I don't want to go home!" she whimpered. "It's so depressing with everything that's happened. I mean, my ex is having his Mom call yours. Your parents probably think I'm trouble."

I shook my head earnestly. "Oh no, they don't judge like that! They make their own decisions, hon. I did tell my Mom it could easily be a simple case of sour grapes, and asked her to give you the benefit of the doubt and make her own decision based on *you*, not what she'd been told."

"I hope that's true. I'm not the bad person his Mom made me out to be."

But of course, she was. Hindsight's 20/20, and looking back, I realize everything my Mom had been told was true—every bit of it. That look in Stacy's eyes wasn't sadness at all; it was fear. She was riddled with guilt, and scared to death she'd be found out before she could sink her hooks into me. She'd never expected the controversy to start so early in our relationship. We'd only been seeing each other three to four days; how did her ex's Mom find out so quickly?

That's what she was worried about; if she was sad about anything, it was the possibility that her meal ticket might get away.

I put my worries behind me. We spent almost every available hour of every day together during that week. On Friday we decided to go walking in another park, which I knew had a park bench overlooking a river. It was a nice, quiet, serene location to just sit, relax, and talk. I can't say I was all that surprised when she eventually asked, "Do you ever think about getting married again?"

I looked at her. "Yes, someday, I suppose," I said honestly. "I like the idea of marriage; I just didn't have a very good experience my first time."

"I don't understand why your ex-wife let you go," she said, snuggling up to me. "I think you'd be a great husband!"

Of course, that made me feel about ten feet tall—just as it was meant to. "Well, I guess you'd have to ask her why. To be honest, I'm not too sure myself what happened. We just kind of drifted apart."

She went on, just as if I hadn't said anything. "I'd like to get married again someday, too. Maybe we'll still be together down the road!"

The bells and whistles should have started going off in my head, but I took her comment as general conversation, and started talking about the strike and wondering how long I'd be out of work. The conversation changed to other things, until we began the walk back to the car and she broached the subject of marriage again. This time I heard the bells starting to clang, and felt the first real tinges of concern. I'd just gotten over a divorce and wasn't looking to jump back in the frying pan; the ink on my divorce papers was still drying. I wasn't looking for 'Miss Right,' just 'Miss Right Now,' and I was quite content with things the way they were. Little did I know that Stacy had other plans; waiting wasn't an option for her at all. She needed someone to financially support her and her kids.

After leaving the park, we stopped by my parents' house so that I could change clothes before we went out to dinner. Stacy spent the time while I was upstairs talking to my Mother and Father; this little diversion gave her the opportunity do some damage control, in an effort to dispel some of the things that had been said to them about her. As I was walking down the stairs back to the living room, I heard her say that she'd never treat me like my ex-wife had. She'd have supper on the table when I came home from work, she'd keep the house spotless, she'd launder my clothes whenever I needed them, etc . . . . It had been less than a week since we'd first laid eyes on each other, and she was discussing marriage with my parents! *Maybe I'm wrong about her,* I mused. *Maybe she's reiterating what she told her ex's parents.*

In retrospect, I realize I should have seen the signs right then—but I was so infatuated with the idea of finding female companionship that I was blinded by her light. Her Mom volunteering to pay for the motel room at the resort, and saying she'd babysit the kids any time Stacy and I wanted to have some quiet time together—those offers should also have caught my attention. Why weren't her kids in school? Spring break was long since past; all of these incidents occurred in March and early April of that year.

Stacy kept hinting about marriage, and soon brought out a calendar and started mentioning dates. I was thinking that if I asked her to marry me, the wedding wouldn't take place until sometime the next summer; however, Stacy had other ideas in mind. She'd already found a house for rent which would allow us to move in together, she said. I informed Stacy that the rent payment was above my financial means at the moment, and that I thought she was rushing things along just a little too fast.

"That's not a problem," she insisted. "I have a job interview on Tuesday of next week; we'll be fine, Jonathan!"

I was confused. "But you already have a job, Stacy. Or do you? I thought you took a vacation day on Monday, but you haven't been back."

She smiled charmingly. "Oh, honey, I'm sorry, I thought I told you; I called and took this whole week off. This new job will be closer to home, and the pay is better!"

The next Tuesday came and went—no interview. "I thought you had an interview today?" I asked her that evening.

"I did," she said in a depressed tone. "They called the day before to inform me the position was no longer available. The director of the nursing facility said someone had turned in their resignation and then recanted at the last minute."

I found that hard to believe. *Something's not right,* I kept telling myself. *Either she's forgetting to tell me these things, which is a problem in itself, or she's making up the answers to each question as I ask them.*

By then, Stacy and her Mom had already decided on a wedding date: only two months away. During another evening of sexual pleasure, I agreed. Later, I was told I'd been too close to the situation and couldn't see the forest for the trees, and I eventually came to the conclusion that this was, in fact, the case. I did feel I was a puppet on a string; she was manipulating me to agree to everything.

I honestly can't say I lost control. I don't believe I ever had it.

4

A Marriage Made in Hell

I would eventually come to see Stacy as a con artist who used manipulation to get her way; it was her preferred method of control. She was only happy when she could pull my strings and make things happen that benefited her and the kids—always them, never me. I wasn't even in the equation. She thrived on conflict and absolutely loved controversy. If there were no current problems, she'd create a crisis of some sort so she could maintain her control.

A reliable co-worker who had attended high school with Stacy told me that my new fiancée had been very popular back then. So why was she still single? Something wasn't clicking, so I did my best to dig up more information on her. My search was fruitless: I was never able to find any hidden skeletons, anywhere. She had very few real friends, and I found myself constantly running into dead ends. Stacy painted a rosy picture of our future together, but I still had my reservations. My entire life I'd always heard that if something sounded too good to be true, then it probably was. I continued in my quest for answers, but couldn't find any closets containing skeletons. If there were any skeletons out there, no one was talking.

The truth, as it turned out, was that people knew her capabilities and the extent of her wrath when crossed, and didn't want to be targeted by her.

Stacy had quickly and accurately deduced that her bedroom talents—which were considerable—were the key to breaking down my reserves. She could get me to agree to almost anything while in the throes of passion. Plus, she was honey-tongued with other people; she continued to work her charms on my parents, despite what her ex's Mom had told them. Even so, it was my parents who first sensed something fishy, who quickly would come to realize that she'd cast a spell over me and was holding me emotionally, mentally and physically hostage. This came fairly early in the relationship, because once she'd sunk her claws into me, she started to alienate me from my friends and family. They tried to talk to me about it; they would inform me of their findings, and deep down I knew it was all true, yet I always defended Stacy and gave her the benefit of the doubt.

I continued my own digging into her past, because something wasn't right and I knew I had to find it. She was finally able to manipulate me into renting the house she'd found earlier, the one I knew was financially above my means. I told her repeatedly I couldn't afford the payments alone, and she always responded the same way: "Jonathan, I promise I'll get a job just as soon as we get back from our honeymoon."

"You're going to have to, Stacy; I can't do it alone."

I'd been working at my current job for twelve years; I made a decent salary, had excellent benefits, and loved what I did. I was well-liked and respected by my co-workers and supervisors. I remember one of my supervisors coming up to me the day before my wedding and wishing me the best. I'll never forget the advice I was given that day: "Life seems to be moving a little fast for you, Jonathan. I hope when the newness wears off and things slow down, you'll find it's the life you really wanted. If it's not, no one will fault you for walking away."

Unbeknownst to me, most of my co-workers thought I was making a terrible mistake. However, out of respect, no one dared approach me about what I was getting into. They'd all been so supportive and encouraging during my divorce; I wish one of them would have said something to me about Stacy, though I'm sure I wouldn't have listened.

The wedding day came and went; none of my co-workers attended. Stacy and I went on a short honeymoon and returned home on Monday. I took a vacation the following week to spend our first week as a married couple with her. I'd convinced myself that once she started working full-time, her enthusiasm in the bedroom would slow down.

I waited until Thursday night of that week to bring up the job search; I hadn't seen or heard any efforts on her part to secure a job. "How's the job search going, Stacy?" I finally asked.

She smiled prettily. "Oh, I forgot to tell you: the Friday before we got married, I got a call asking me to come in for an interview this week. I told them I was getting married the next day and we were on vacation this week, so they're going to call back next Tuesday."

I wasn't charmed. "You said you were going to look for a job this week!"

"I know I did, honey, but I'd much rather spend my first married week with my new husband. You took vacation this week, didn't you?"

I signed. "Yes. I did. But I have a job, and I'm being paid for this week. You're not."

'Honey, please don't worry, okay?" she said plaintively. "I *said* I'm going to take care of you."

I rolled my eyes, frustrated. "Stacy, my *Mom* took care of me. I need someone to help me financially, emotionally, and sexually."

"Jonathan, I told you, I'll be here for you." It never occurred to me at the time, but as it turned out, this was one of the few times she actually told me the truth; she really *was* always 'there' for me. She was always at home, lying in wait!

I sighed. "Stacy, I'm sorry, but I can't help but feel concerned. Financially, I can't do everything to keep us afloat, and I'm afraid I'll wear myself down. This is supposed to be one of the happiest times in my life, but we've only been married five days and I feel like I'm already in over my head and sinking."

"Everything will be okay," she insisted, snuggling up to me. She'd cleverly accomplished her goal; she'd avoided searching for a job the week after the honeymoon, and soon, that week stretched into a month. She used sex as a means to pacify me every time I brought the subject up.

By then she was spending a lot of money. I'd made a major mistake early on when I left her in charge of paying the bills. She'd buy everything that she or her kids needed or wanted first, and what was left over was doled out to bills. It wasn't enough. To my shock and embarrassment, bill collectors started to call me at work. I'd never had to deal with anything like that before; I'd always paid my bills promptly, and (until then) had excellent credit. The stress started to get to me. I made up my mind to approach her about my concerns, and decided I wasn't going to let her distract me with sex this time.

I came home from work one evening after having a very bad day, but still determined to talk her about our financial situation. She assailed me as soon as I came in the front door. She was completely enraged; I'd never see this side of her before. It turned out that she had maxed out my credit card at the department store where I always shopped for clothes. "Do you know how *embarrassing* it is to be standing at the register with people behind you in line, only to be told by the cashier the credit card was denied?" she demanded. "I want you to call the store and report the clerk for being rude and unprofessional! Are you going to let them embarrass me like that, Jonathan?"

I'd sat down on the couch by then, and she stood over me with a cordless phone in her hand, waiting for me to take it. "Come on, call them now! I can't believe you're going to let them get away with it! All I have to say is, you don't love *me*, you just married me for the sex!"

I wasn't as thoroughly cowed as she'd thought. "Stacy, have you lost your damned mind?" I exploded. "I'm not calling them; *you're* the one who maxed out the card, and *you're* the one who didn't pay the bill. If you want to spend money like water, then get a job and *make* some! I've told you before and I'll tell you again: I can't do it all. I. Need. Your. Help!"

When she saw I wasn't going to be a pushover this time, she knew she had to change her tactics to break me down; so she switched sides and played defense. Her tone changed from angry and assertive to calm and supportive, as her voice became much softer. "Look, I know it's not your fault, honey. I know you're doing all you can, and I promise I'm going to help you. I know you try! You're so good to me!"

Her facial expressions and the movements of her hands were indicating she wanted to go to her lair, the bedroom. She was merely playing a game; if Mrs. Hyde didn't get the job done, Dr. Jekyll would always come through. It made absolutely no difference to her which role she had to play, as long as she accomplished her goal. I had no idea then how often I'd be seeing Mrs. Hyde, and actually came to miss the Jekyll side of her personality.

"Oh, honey, please call and see if they'll increase your credit limit. I saw some *really* cute things today. They have this buy one/ get one half price sale in the Lingerie department. You should see all the pretty new stuff they have. It's so *sexy*, Jonny! Please call and see about a limit increase for me; please!" Her last comments were made with a pouting look on her face—and she was still urging me towards the bedroom.

I caved. I knew that if I didn't make the call and make some mild comment about the clerk, plus ask for a credit line increase, I'd be in for a night of hell. I was tired and had already had a very bad day, even before coming home. Truth be told, I didn't want sex; I only wanted to go to bed and sleep. But maybe if I made the call, she'd leave me alone. So I went against my better judgment and made the call, just to pacify her.

When I hung up the phone I said to her tiredly, "They increased the credit limit by two hundred dollars."

"Oh! Thank you so much, sweetie! You'll be so *excited* when you see what I can buy and wear just for you!"

She'd gotten me to do exactly what she wanted, as usual; all it took was a little manipulation and control. By then, she'd developed a way to use sex both ways: she'd give it to me to get what she wanted, or she'd threaten to retain it if I didn't let her have her way. She didn't care which game she had to play, as long as she got her way. She was a real professional that way.

My co-workers began seeing me differently, and they didn't like the change. I couldn't do my job efficiently anymore, and I had trouble concentrating. Once, I'd been jovial and humorous; now I'd transformed into Mr. Doom-and-Gloom. They liked the old me, but didn't know what to think of the person who inhabited my body now.

Looking back, I'll always remember the phone call I received at work on a Monday at lunch time; we'd been married about six months by then, and she used the opportunity to successfully orchestrate one of her craftiest manipulations to date. My phone had already rung at least ten times that day. She'd probably accounted for nine of those calls—and the day was only half over. I knew my co-workers were counting the phone calls. I noticed that every time I received a call, a guy across the room would make a little pencil mark on the counter top. I'd also noticed that when I wasn't on the phone, people were moving around and doing their usual work; but when my phone rang, their activities seemed to stop completely. They acted like they were deeply concentrating on their work, but I knew they were listening.

I answered the phone to hear: "I need you to wait until next week to pay the light bill. I need money to buy clothes for work!"

I cheered up at the thought. "Did someone call? Do you have an interview?"

"No, but I'll need the clothes to work."

"Stacy, when you get a job, we'll go out and get you some new clothes."

"I need new clothes to start work. What if I get a call and they want me to start tomorrow?"

"Stacy, you haven't applied for any jobs, and I seriously doubt anyone is going to call this afternoon wanting you to start work tomorrow," I responded calmly. "But if by some chance it happens, you can wear something you have, and we'll go shopping this weekend."

"I want something new to wear on my first day! Do you want your wife to go to work dressed like she shops at a secondhand store?"

"Stacy, you have nice clothes hanging in the closet. Wear the dress you wore on our honeymoon. You get the job, and then I'll buy the clothes; end of discussion."

"Okay, Jonathan, have it your way! Don't come home giving me a rash of shit if I turn down a really good job offer because I don't have decent clothes to wear to an interview so I can make a good impression."

I remember losing my cool at that point, and raising my voice. Of course, my co-workers were eating it up. "Stacy, let me explain it to you again, okay? There are *no* high-paying employers picking random numbers out of the phone book, looking to fill job positions. The only way you'll get a call is to actually get your ass off the couch and go apply for a job!"

She shouted, "Now you listen to what I'm telling *you*, okay? I don't have the clothes to go out and apply at good-paying companies!"

"Stacy; you don't *need* new clothes, you need nursing uniforms, and I don't think I've ever heard that fashion was any aspect of a nursing career."

"But I don't *want* to go back to nursing," she whined. "I want something more professional, so I can wear dresses, hosiery and heels everyday; I know how much you'd like that!"

I ground my teeth and rubbed my brow . . . not that it helped. "Stacy, at this point, a job flipping hamburgers would be fine," I snapped. "It pays money! Lying your ass on the sofa all day doesn't! If you make an effort, I'll help you."

"Are you going to give me the money or not?"

"No! I *told* you to get the job first!"

"Go screw yourself!" she said, and hung up.

I knew my co-workers were enjoying this. I'd already heard the jokes about the "Stacy Show," and we'd just provided them with a brand new episode.

I sat staring down at my desk. I didn't want to look at anyone. I tried to act as if the call didn't bother me, and busied myself with something on the desktop. I knew there would be smirks on their faces if I turned around. Things had escalated to the point where I couldn't even look my long-term friends and colleagues in the eye anymore—I felt so deeply ashamed at the person I'd become.

On the other hand, I was also guilt-ridden about the way I'd talked to Stacy. I knew I was right, but I felt so damned guilty! She was *that* good. She'd planted a seed, and knew I'd think about it. I started envisioning her coming home from work in nice dresses and skirts, high heels and hosiery. The more I thought, the more I realized she presented a good point; she *would* need nice work clothes. I resigned myself to giving in.

That afternoon, I used some money I'd been hiding in my car, and made a $150 payment on the department store account on the way home from work.

Yes, by then I'd resorted to hiding money in my car. Stacy had started going through my wallet, without my knowledge, while I was sleeping. I'd found out in a uniquely embarrassing way. I'd stopped one night at a Taco Bell on my way to work the 12-8 shift, placed my order, and drove to the window to pay. When I opened my wallet, all the money was gone. It was extremely embarrassing to tell the cashier that my wife had taken the money from my wallet. She must have felt sympathy; she voided the order but gave me the food anyway. I told her I'd bring the money the next night if she was going to be there, and I did.

When I arrived home from work after the brand new episode of the Stacy Show went out, I told Stacy I'd made a payment and that she could buy her clothes the next day. She was ecstatic. In my mind, I trusted her to do what she said; I don't know why. In her mind, of course, she'd just gotten a $150 shopping spree from her sugar daddy, and had no intentions of buying work clothes. She would buy things to use against me, sexy lingerie in particular. She had no intention of looking for employment either. Her philosophy went along the lines of, "Why buy the pig, when all you want is a little sausage?"

When I arrived home from work the next day, she met me at the front door with a glass of iced tea. "Sit on the couch, enjoy your tea, and relax for a few minutes!" she said happily. "You're going to need your strength tonight, honey!"

She went into the bedroom, and came out five minutes later wearing new red lingerie. She reached out, took my hand, and practically pulled me into the bedroom.

Afterwards, I asked to see the work clothes she'd bought. She showed me lots of lingerie, but nothing else. To put it mildly, I was incensed. "*This* is what you bought for work, Stacy? Where do you plan on working—at a strip club, swinging from a damned pole?"

"I didn't see anything I liked," she pouted.

"Then why didn't you wait? Why did you buy all lingerie?"

"I can use this for work, too."

I sighed. "Yes, I'm sorry. You're right, Stacy. You're always right. You can wear the new stuff under your old clothes. If anyone says anything about how poorly you're dressed, if they ask if you shop at a secondhand store, you can take your clothes off and show them your new underwear! You'll really show *them*, won't you?"

I was so damn mad I could have choked the living hell out of her—and she knew it. So of course she switched gears. The look she gave me was one of defeat. It was part of her plan, to let me think I'd won; and it was something new in her arsenal (or new to me, at least), so I fell for it, at least partially. "You're right, honey," she muttered. "I wasn't thinking. It's just . . . I enjoy our sex life so much, I always want to look desirable for you!"

I sighed and embraced her. "All right, all right. So what's for supper?"

She frowned. "I've been shopping all day, and I'm so *tired*. Can't we go out to eat?"

Instantly, I was furious again. "No! We don't have the money! What little bit I *did* have saved you just spent!"

"But . . . can't you write a check at the grocery store? We need a few things anyway, and you can write it for $50 over."

I stared at her. "Where the hell am I going to get the money to pay for the groceries and the fifty extra dollars?"

"It takes three days for the check to get to the bank, and you get paid Friday."

"Stacy, it's only *Monday*!"

She smiled tightly. "Everything will be all right. Don't worry, Jonny! I'll borrow some money from my Mom to put into the bank and you can pay her back Friday. I'll get dressed to go out. Is it too cold to wear my short skirt and the heels you like? Oh, I wasn't thinking . . ." She looked at me with a sultry expression. "My pantyhose will keep my legs warm, won't they?"

She saw it in my eyes: she knew I loved those legs in hose and heels. She threw out the bait and I swallowed it. She knew she'd won when I made my next comment: "So, if I pay your Mom back on Friday, how do I pay the phone and light bill?"

"I'll call and make arrangements with them," she said cheerfully. Damn, she was beautiful, and so very, very sexy. "Now . . . I want you to be thinking about the lingerie I bought today, and you choose what I wear when we get back home. Unless, of course, you don't want to fool around tonight. I was thinking that on the way home after eating I can get you in the mood in the car . . . no one will see me with my head in your lap, if you take the back roads. You might want to drive slowly, though!"

She knew she'd just put the icing on the cake.

By the time I'd put up with Stacy's manipulation games for over two years, she'd probably worked a total of two weeks. She did manage to land the occasional job here and there—more to shut me up than anything else—but any excuse would make her call in sick. If her son or daughter had a sniffle, she called in and said her child was very sick and she wouldn't be coming in. Sure, the sex was good—but by no means was the one hour of sex worth the other twenty-three hours of hell I had to deal with every day. Her job searches and interviews never amounted to much, and I frankly have no idea how she managed to be so lazy without going totally insane with boredom.

Her part of the social contract meant nothing to her. It got to the point there was never any supper waiting when I came home; dirty clothes were lying all over the house. We had to move four times over the first two years, because I couldn't afford to pay the rent. My credit score dropped like a rock. I soon had several judgments against me from former landlords, and I'd made arrangements to pay them to keep my wages from being garnished. I was constantly receiving letters from collection companies. I wasn't aware how bad my credit had gotten, though, until I applied for a new car loan and was turned down flat. I'd never had a problem getting loans at my credit union, and I went in to inquire as to why I'd been refused. Their advice was to get a copy of my credit report.

My relationship with my parents was also faltering; they knew that every time I called, I needed money.

On top of all that, my job performance was suffering. I'd get calls at three o'clock in the morning from other shifts, telling me I'd made major mistakes on the job. It was hard to concentrate on work with Stacy constantly calling for ridiculous reasons. I'd already been counseled by my boss for abusing the telephone during work hours. It had gotten so bad that he answered my phone for me one day, and told her in no uncertain terms to stop calling so often. Once or twice a shift was fine, he'd said, but not every thirty or forty minutes! She responded to his suggestion by calling the personnel department the next day and making a formal complaint. She lied, saying she'd called me with a family emergency and my boss refused to put me on the phone.

I also came to realize that I was neglecting my son; I rarely even saw him anymore. I had to hear from Carrie, my first wife, about how my marriage to Stacy was destroying the bond between my son and me. Then there was the time I was talking to him, and he referred to his step-father as "Dad." Damn, that really hurt. I knew being around Stacy wasn't a good environment for him, so I tried to limit their encounters. This was fine with him, as he didn't want to be around her, but the principle effect was to strain our father-son relationship almost to the breaking point.

Then there was the child-support issue. I'd always felt I had an obligation to help take care of my boy, so Carrie and I had agreed that I'd have child support funds transferred from my checking account to hers at the first of every month. Stacy's spending habits wrecked that. She caused me to get behind, and my child support payments were getting later with each passing month. After I'd gotten over a month behind, my ex-wife turned it over to Child Support Enforcement Services, and after that the money was taken directly from my paychecks—just like I was some kind of dead-beat dad who didn't give a damn for his offspring.

I thought for sure that conditions couldn't get any worse. I was so naïve.

5

Are We Having Fun Yet?

In the early years of our marriage, it soon became obvious to me that Stacy was dependent on prescription drugs, particularly Xanax. I tried to get her to cut back on the drugs, but she'd just snarl at me and refuse. It seemed she needed them to get through even the most minor of life's crises, and it wasn't long before she was eating them like candy.

Early one morning, while working the 12 to 8 shift, I started having chest pains about two hours before quitting time. I'd been having the pains on and off for over a week, but they'd never been as bad as they were this time. I knew it was stress-related; but just to be sure, I stopped by my doctor's office on the way home that morning. They ran an EKG and determined I was having panic attacks. The doctor prescribed 0.5 mg of Xanax, and instructed me to only take them if I really felt I needed to. I really wished the doctor had prescribed something else, because now Stacy had another means of obtaining Xanax—me.

He only prescribed thirty pills, and Stacy used them up in two days. I wasn't aware she'd taken them until the next day, when I had another attack and noticed my pills were gone. After she'd depleted both her supply and mine, I was given a choice: I could call my doctor and ask for refills, or I could take her to the ER. I refused to do either one, and was rewarded with both a barrage of obscenities and Stacy's newly-acquired form of intimidation: destruction of property.

I never completely understood why, but if someone pissed Stacy off on the telephone, she'd throw the phone at the walls. It didn't necessarily have to be me on the other end of the line to make her angry; it might be one of the kids, her Mom, or even a telemarketer who just happened to call at a bad time. It was never her oldest son, however; he rarely called or gave her any trouble. I really liked him; he was the complete opposite of the two at home. He was respectful to his Mother no matter the circumstances, and he maintained a full time job, enabling him to support himself and his girlfriend. When I explained her newest tendency to him, he told me that throwing the phones was her way of expressing anger. "Hell, I knew that already!" I told him.

After she'd broken all the phones in the house, I refused to buy any more. So she'd borrow money from someone and purchase them herself. You'd think she'd learn, but she didn't; this activity continued for close to six months. I have no idea how many telephones were destroyed during that time, but I do know that the average lifespan of a telephone in our household was about a week. I tried reasoning with her by explaining that the phone was only a tool used to relay information from the person on the other end, and much to my surprise, she finally listened; but only, I think, because her Mother had taken ill, and she needed to stay in close contact with her.

Phones were eventually taken off the endangered species list, but she found other household items to vent her frustrations on, particularly ashtrays, drinking glasses and knick-knacks. After those, it escalated to kitchen chairs and kitchen drawers. It seemed she couldn't tolerate seeing a kitchen drawer in its place; it looked so much better lying on the floor with the contents scattered all over the kitchen.

I began seriously questioning why I continued to stay in this environment, and soon realized it was time to seek professional help. My employer offered counseling for employees who felt they needed to talk to someone about work-related or personal issues, so I took advantage of the service. The only problem was that the counselor was there only one afternoon a week. With over a thousand employees, it was very difficult to get in on the spur of the moment. My supervisor knew I was deeply troubled, however, and he personally called Medical to schedule an appointment for me.

Luckily, he discovered that she had an opening in ten minutes for a thirty minute session, and I took advantage of it. I told her as much as possible in the allotted time, and when I was done, she explained that her sessions were more designed for quick-fix issues and strongly advised I seek continuous treatment by a licensed therapist or clinical psychologist outside of the workplace. I called my insurance provider later that day, and they set up an appointment for me with a therapist near my home on my next off day.

When I went in for my first visit, the therapist introduced himself and asked what he could do to help me; "Tell me why you're here!" he said. He probably wished he'd never given me the opportunity to lead off the conversation, because I talked incessantly, filling up the fifty-minute session with as much information as I possibly could. He'd barely gotten a word in edgewise during the visit, but I noticed he took lots of notes and appeared to be very intrigued by my history with Stacy; I secretly wondered if he thought I had a death wish. Towards the end of the appointment, he said my situation seemed very complex, and it would take quite a while to come to a resolution. I asked if I could set up weekly appointments, to which he agreed; however, he suggested I schedule an appointment with a psychiatrist in the practice he worked for, and helped me in setting up the appointment. He also decided I should be on medication for depression.

The therapist was amazed at how much I'd taken from Stacy—yet I was still with her, and that was something I couldn't explain. I'm sure in a strange, twisted sort of way I loved her, but superficially, she'd become a demon, spawned from Satan himself. I was no longer able to see the attraction that had initially drawn me towards her; she quickly sensed this. Our sex life had slowed considerably at this point, which gave her a new subject to dwell on. Since there had to be a crisis of some type in her life, she assumed I was having an affair.

By then Stacy and I had just celebrated our first anniversary of marital hell, and she'd still not found employment.

I was in a department store one afternoon, and had a chance encounter with Stacy's ex-boyfriend, Paul. He supplied me with a very limited amount of information about his and Stacy's relationship. He was reluctant to say anything, as I was still married to her; but the story he told me was public knowledge, so he figured there was no harm.

After exchanging some small talk, Paul asked, "Are you still with Stacy?"

"Yeah . . . I can't seem to break the spell she has over me. I just can't explain it, man. How did you do it?"

"I made up my mind to get away when she pulled a crafty maneuver with my credit card. She charged clothing for her kids, and put me at my limit."

"Yeah, well, she's kept mine at the limit too."

"Well, here's what she did to me. I gave her money to go pay the bill, and she'd pay it all right—and then she'd charge it back up again. So the next month I'd give her money again, and she'd pay the bill and charge it back up again. After we'd broken it off, she even took me to court for some personal items her Mom had given me to decorate my apartment; they wanted the items back."

I nodded wearily. "Yeah, I think I remember something about her taking you to court."

Paul snorted in disgust. "She screwed me good, is what she did. I countersued to recover the money she'd purchased on my credit card since I'd given her the money to make the payments. But she lied and said she'd made the payments with her own money, and produced the receipts. I couldn't believe she'd kept them. Well, there was no way I could prove I'd given her the money, and since she had the receipts, the judge ruled in her favor. Then my family was sent a letter from an attorney telling us not to try to contact her in any way. By that time, she was seeing you. I eventually had to file for bankruptcy because of her."

"Damn, she's definitely a manipulative woman." I sighed.

"Jonathan, my advice to you is to be *very careful*. She and her Mother are always planning something. If you have an opportunity to get out, take it. Run like hell and don't look back!"

It was a strange coincidence I'd run into Paul that day, because as it happened, I would very soon have the opportunity to get out.

I was working the 8 to 4 shift one week and knew there'd be overtime on the weekend, so I informed her I was going to work over onto the 4 to 12 shifts both Friday and Saturday night. By then, I was in dire straits for money to pay the bills. Coincidently, my Mom had increased her frequency of phone calls; she was concerned about my health since the panic attacks had begun. She'd always ask questions which only required a 'yes' or 'no' answer, so that's all I needed to say. Stacy's insecure mind, however, thought my Mom and I were plotting something against her, and so devised a plot to go out of town with the kids while I worked overtime. She went back to the city in which she'd lived with the husband who'd died; she had a friend there, whom I'd met at our wedding. To the best of my knowledge, this was the only friend Stacy had. Stacy had called me both of those nights at work to verify that I was indeed working over, and then she'd allow me ample time to get home before calling me again.

"What are you doing?" she'd ask.

"I'm getting ready for bed."

"How did the overtime go?"

"Good. It was a very quiet night."

"So who's there with you?"

"Nobody's here! That's a stupid question, Stacy."

"Well, a friend of mine called and said she saw you with a woman in your car earlier tonight!"

"How'd she call you if you're not at home?"

"Oh, um, did I say she called me? I meant to say, I called her, and she told me then."

"Yeah, okay, Stacy. You haven't talked to her in months, but out of nowhere you get the sudden urge to call her while you're out of town? Didn't you call me at work tonight?"

A brief silence, then, "Yes, I did."

"Did I talk to you on the phone the times you *did* call?"

"Yes."

"Okay, then, use your head. How could I have been out with another woman in my car, if you called me at work twice and I was there both times and talked to you?"

"You tell me!"

I rolled my eyes. "Look, Stacy. It's late, and I have to be back at work at eight in the morning; I don't have time for your insecurity games."

"So are you telling me you *didn't* have a woman in the car with you earlier?"

"Correct, Stacy; I was at work until midnight."

"Then why didn't you call me?"

"I didn't have to. *You* kept calling *me*, remember? Now, look. I'm tired and want to go to sleep. I don't have time to reinforce your insecurities. You should have stayed home if you wanted to keep tabs on me. Now, goodnight!"

Two weeks later, while lying in the bed, I noticed that Stacy had that faraway look on her face again. "What's wrong with you?" I asked. I didn't really want to know, but felt I should at least ask.

"I made a mistake," she admitted.

"Only one?" I said sarcastically.

"I'm serious, Jonathan, I made a mistake!" There were actually tears in her eyes.

I sighed heavily. "Okay, what did you do now?"

"I said I made a mistake, a big one." This time she sounded sullen, and I was at the end of my patience.

"All right, Stacy, I think we've established the fact that you made a mistake. Now, what was the mistake, dammit?"

"Remember the night I called and asked if you had a girl in your car?"

"Yes, the night I worked over. One of them, anyway."

"You said you never called where I was."

"That's right, I didn't call, you kept calling me."

"Well, if you would have called, I wouldn't have been at my friend's. I was out until after eleven."

"You and your friend?"

"No; just me!"

"And . . . ?"

She lowered her head. "Remember the guy I told you about that was so nice to me when my last husband died? He was his boss, remember me telling you?"

"Let me guess. You were with *him*." I was more tired than angry at that point; she'd already put me through so much that this was hardly a surprise.

"Yes . . ." she said almost inaudibly.

"So at least one of the phone calls you made to me at work came from his place?"

"Yes!"

Obviously, Stacy had let her own insecurities convince her I was the one having an affair; so she had one to get even with me. I looked at her and said, "So how did this happen, Stacy? Did you go down there with an affair in mind, or was it coincidental?"

"It was an accident. Jill and I went to the mall with all the kids, and he saw me and came over to talk. He asked how I was doing, and invited me to dinner to talk over old times." She fell silent so long I felt the need to prompt her.

"And . . . ?"

"I told him I'd remarried, and didn't think it would be appropriate to go to dinner with him. He said he understood, and then asked if I'd like to come by his apartment later just to talk . . . so I agreed."

I turned away. "Stacy, that's the dumbest shit I've ever heard. You refused dinner in a public restaurant because you're married, but agreed to meet him at his apartment alone?"

" . . . Yes, it was stupid."

"Did you walk around the mall with a sign on your back saying 'I want to have an affair'? Because you might as well have."

"I know," she said sadly, "and I'm sorry. One thing lead to another, things got carried away, and the next thing I knew, we were in his bedroom. If it makes you feel any better, I cried the whole time!"

I glared at her. "Gee, Stacy, that makes me feel a whole lot better," I snarled. "Do you actually expect me to believe that bullshit story? You're telling me you'd have a guilty conscience going to dinner in public, but being in a man's apartment wasn't a problem? You just answered my question. You went there with an affair on your mind! And you cried the whole time, you poor, poor thing. Does it make me feel any better? Hell, no; that has got to be the stupidest thing you've ever said."

"I did *not* go there with an affair on my mind!"

"Then *why did you go to his apartment?* Why not go to the restaurant instead? What the hell was he supposed to think? What was *I* supposed to think?"

"I told you I made a big mistake, didn't I?" she cried.

"Yes, that's what you said; but you left out the most important part of the story!"

"Go to hell!"

"You *wanted* to make the mistake."

"I didn't intend to . . . ."

I cut her off in mid-sentence. My voice was calm, icy. "Stacy, darling, it happened *exactly* the way you wanted it to. You didn't go to dinner because you wanted to go to his apartment and have sex with him. You knew it, he knew it, and I know it now. You wanted to take revenge on the affair that you'd created in your mind, the one you decided I was having."

The look on her face told me I was right. She wasn't dumb; she knew exactly what she was doing.

I wasn't as upset as I thought I would be, but I'd be lying if I said I wasn't hurt by her confession, especially since I was the one always being accused of cheating. I'd had to live through the accusations without at least getting the fun that came with it. Afterward, we went to marriage counseling at her request. I sat and listened to her boo-hoo through a month of therapy. I couldn't tell if she was being honest and sincere or simply acting; I was torn between the two possibilities. I even considered the possibility that she'd made the whole story up to see if I'd retaliate and sleep with another woman as payback. If so, she was a ruthless bitch; no surprise there. The other choice, of course, was that she had to be telling the truth. I just couldn't fathom anyone like her admitting to having an affair out of the blue and then going through weeks of marriage counseling if it was all an act. She could have lost me forever, which was one hell of a gamble if it was all an invention. If she was acting, she deserved an award!

Years later, she tried to convince me it *wasn't* true, and she'd made the whole story up. In my opinion, it would take a cold-hearted woman to put a man through the pain and humiliation of going to marriage counseling just to see if I'd retaliate. I doubt I'll ever know the truth.

During our second year of marriage, I woke up one evening prior to working the 12-8 shift and Stacy was simply elated. She'd gone out that afternoon, and run into a friend she went to nursing school with. The friend was an administrator at a nursing home; she offered Stacy a job, and she accepted. To me it felt like Christmas in July! *Finally,* I thought, *finally, relief may be in sight.* Stacy's Mom even volunteered to take her out the next day and buy her some uniforms to wear.

Stacy's first assignment was to work one week on the 3-11 shift. After she'd worked two complete days, I thought things might be looking up, that there was hope after all. On Stacy's third day, I'd woken up early, so I got out of bed and went downstairs; her son, Shawn, was playing Nintendo. "Where's Suzy?" I asked.

He glanced at me disinterestedly. "Not sure; she got into an argument with her boyfriend on the phone and I haven't seen her since."

I went back upstairs, but she wasn't in her room. I looked out the front door to see if she was on the porch, and noticed right away that something was missing; my car wasn't in the driveway.

"Shawn, did Suzy take my car?"

"Well, I wasn't supposed to say anything, but yeah, she did. She said she'd be back before you got up."

"How the hell did she get my car keys?"

He shrugged. "She snuck into the room while you were asleep and took them from your pants pocket."

"Did she ask permission from your Mother before she left?"

"Well, she called and asked, but Mom said no."

Suzy had been driving a little over a year, but I didn't allow her to drive my car, ever. It was just too much engine for her.

I called the nursing home and left a message for Stacy to call home when she took a break. She called within thirty minutes, and I told her that Suzy had taken my car without permission and gone to her boyfriend's, which was about an hour away. Stacy went ballistic at work, and started screaming and yelling; she was a nervous wreck. I had this vivid picture in my head of Stacy throwing a fit at the nurse's station while all the residents in wheelchairs sat and watched. She called her friend the administrator and said she had a family emergency and had to leave.

Before Stacy could arrive home, the boyfriend's Dad had driven Suzy and the car back; his wife followed in their own car so they could get home. They'd no sooner left than Stacy showed up, completely out of control.

The next morning, Stacy's administrator friend called and told her in no uncertain terms that her employment had been terminated. The elderly residents told tales of Stacy throwing things and yelling; worse, she'd left her position without being relieved.

At the suggestion of my therapist, I decided I needed to try to be more assertive towards Stacy, to threaten to take the control away from her. I immediately went home and told her I refused to be controlled and manipulated anymore. "Life is too short for this bullshit!" I declared. Naturally; Stacy blamed it all on the therapist; she said he'd filled my head up with nonsense.

I didn't agree, and I still don't. I put my plan into action, and attempted to put an end to her controlling ways. One of the more prominent episodes occurred during the third year of our struggling marriage. Shawn had decided he was going to his girlfriend's house after school. He was only 11 or 12 at the time, but to hear him talk, they were "dating." Both Stacy and I agreed he wasn't going; I'd be there at the end of the school day, and pick him up as usual. He later called Stacy at home, about thirty minutes before school ended for the day, and again asked—to which she adamantly answered no. She said I'd be there to pick him up. When I arrived at the school that afternoon, of course, Shawn wasn't waiting outside—and he still hadn't appeared after ten minutes. I walked into the school's office to inquire about him, and found him sitting there. I informed the principle that I had been sitting outside waiting for him for some time.

"I'm sorry, Mr. David, but we can't let you take him home," the principal said, refusing to look me in the eyes.

"Is he in trouble for something?" I asked, confused.

"No, sir. We're waiting for Social Services to arrive, and they'll handle the situation."

"I don't understand. What situation are you referring to?"

"Please come back into my office, Mr. David, and I'll explain things to you."

I followed the principal, and looked at my stepson; he had a look of utter confusion on his face.

When I sat down in the chair in front of the principal, he finally looked at me grimly and said, "Mr. David, your stepson came to us this afternoon and made some rather serious accusations."

"Such as?"

"He said that your wife repeatedly drags him out of the bed in the mornings, while beating him."

"*What?* He said that?"

"Yes, sir, he did."

"Well, I can tell you that's completely untrue."

"Mr. David, our guidelines clearly state that when a child makes an accusation of that nature, we have to investigate and notify the proper authorities immediately. He said his mother was picking him up, and, well, and we couldn't allow that to happen. I asked him if there was someone else who could pick him up, and he said there wasn't. However, he did say his girlfriend's Mother had said she'd take him in for a while."

I shook my head sadly. It was all starting to make sense now. Stacy had taught him well; live and learn, as they say. "I know it doesn't matter what I say," I told the principal wearily, "but I can assure you his accusations are completely false." I went on to explain the events that had started that morning, and the follow-up phone call that afternoon.

The principal didn't look particularly surprised. When I was done, I told him, "Okay, I'll let his mother handle this; I'll just take him home and explain to her what he said."

"I'm sorry, Mr. David, but I can't allow that to happen either."

"Why not?" I asked, confused again.

The principal looked away. "Because . . . he accused you of something, too. He said you intentionally burn him with cigarettes on his behind and legs."

"He said that? You have *got* to be kidding me!"

"No, Mr. David, I'm sorry to say I'm not. Now, we did have the school nurse have him undress, and there were no such burn marks on him—so I'm inclined to believe your story."

"Let me take him on home, and my wife and I will handle this!"

The principal sighed. "I wish I could, Mr. David, but it's not that easy. Now, after talking to you, I see his motivation. He was bound and determined to go to his girlfriend's after school, so he fabricated the whole story."

"That's exactly right! So what do we do now?"

"Can you get your wife to come to the school?"

"I'll have to go and get her. It'll take ten or fifteen minutes."

When I got back home, Stacy wanted to know where Shawn was, and I told her I'd explain on the way to the school. After convincing her he hadn't been hurt, she got into the car and I explained. She was more pissed than I was. Social Services had arrived by the time we returned. The social worker introduced herself to us, and we had to listen to the spiel about a certain protocol that had to be followed, and how he wouldn't be released to either of us.

"Is there anyone else who could pick him up and take care of him until this investigation is finished?" the Social Services representative asked.

"My girlfriend's Mom can come get me!" Shawn piped up.

"I'll call his older brother," Stacy said. "Shawn can stay with him for a while."

"That would be ideal," said the social worker.

"But I don't want to go to *his* house. I want to go to my girlfriend's house," Shawn said plaintively.

"It's not your choice!" Stacy snapped, with evil in her eyes.

Stacy's soon-to-be daughter-in-law worked close by, so she came and picked Shawn up and took him to the apartment she shared with Stacy's oldest son, Steven. Stacy and I were closely scrutinized for a week about our housekeeping manners, the food supply, our lifestyle and many other issues before the case was dismissed as false.

When it was time for Shawn to come home from his brother's, Stacy asked me to please be nice. "Try to remember, he's only a child," she said.

"Child, my ass!" I replied. "Anybody who'll go to the lengths he did just to go to his girlfriend's house needs to have his ass beat. I'll be damned if I'm going to sit here and be nice. I'm surprised you don't have any resentment for what he did to you and me! We were child abusers in the eyes of the school staff and Social Services, until we were proven otherwise. That's not the way it's supposed to work in this country!"

"Well, Jonny, his brother has been on him pretty hard for what he did, and I'd say he's suffered enough!"

"Then you're a fool. If that's the way you want to look at it, fine, it's your choice. But I'm not kissing his ass, and I think it would be best if I just don't say anything to him at all."

When Shawn arrived home that day, Stacy ran to hug and kiss him when he came in the door. "I've missed you so much!" she said.

He looked at me and smiled. I just stared back. "Hi, Dad!" he said, to which I just lifted my hand in a sort of wave and never uttered a word. Stacy went with him to his bedroom, and then came back into the kitchen where I was sitting at the table. "I can't believe you!" she said to me. "He spoke to you and even called you Dad. You didn't have the decency to even speak."

I stared at her. "Stacy, I'm going to say this one time. Don't expect me to be nice after he went to the school and accused me of burning him with cigarettes just to get to his girlfriend's. I can tell you this: if he were my child, I'd whip his ass, so it would be best if you just left me alone right now."

We argued most of the evening about my refusal to kiss up to Shawn. I packed up some things and left the next day, but I was back soon. The separations never lasted more than two or three days, tops. I'd always get drawn back by an unknown force. Stacy would turn on her charm; coupled with her magnetic personality and promises that she'd seen the error of her ways, the black widow was able to lure her prey back into the web again. I couldn't break the spell she had over me. I still don't know why.

We had another bad argument a couple months later, and I left again. This time, I broke tradition; I didn't return in the usual two days. It was during this separation that I realized the truth about her parents. I remembered their joy at the news that Stacy and I were going to marry; they had quickly given us their blessings. I'd always thought they liked me, not only as a son-in-law but as a person. I really shouldn't use the term 'her parents'; it was mainly her Mother I should be referring to. I liked Stacy's Dad; he seemed to be sympathetic and understanding, and the more I talked to him, the better I understood that he'd been kept in the dark and didn't know half of what had occurred between Stacy and me.

I'd been gone a week when Stacy's Mom called me at work. "Jonathan, how are you doing?"

I sighed. "I'm doing okay, considering everything that's happened."

"When are you going back home? You should have never left her and them kids there like you did. What's wrong with you?"

"I can't do it all alone, Agnes. You and I have had this conversation before. She needs to get a damn job and help me. What would happen if I got sick? We'd lose everything, that's what. There's no sense in her lying around the house all day when she's fully capable of getting a job. When my checks come in, we fight because I try to pay the bills. She'd rather go out on shopping sprees, spend money on the kids, and then pay bills with what's left—which is usually nothing."

"Well, she called me today wanting me to bring her money. You left them there with no money and food. You should be ashamed of yourself, Jonathan!"

"I *left* there with no money!"

"You've got food at your parent's house; don't try to tell me you're not eating!"

"I'm didn't say I wasn't eating. I said I left there with nothing but pocket change."

"Well, you need to take some money out there so them kids can eat!"

"Where am I supposed to get this money?"

"That's not my problem; you married her under the condition that you would take care of her."

"And she married me with the promise that she'd work to help me! I'm eating because my parents are providing it. Maybe you should invite them to stay at *your* house and *you* can feed them!"

"They ain't coming here, I can't handle it! Your parents could give you some food to take out there!"

"Why? They didn't marry her; I did! I've upheld my end of the deal. I work every day and I take any available overtime. Stacy hasn't upheld her promises; that's not my parents' concern. You talk to her and tell her to get a damn job!"

"She won't listen to me!

"Then you call my parents and tell them they should be taking food out there for them to eat."

"I'm not going to do that!"

"And I'm not either! Until I see some effort on her part, I'm staying right here—and when we get evicted, they can come to your house!"

Suddenly, she relented. "Okay, Jonathan. If I help you get your bills under control, will you go back?"

"I'll give it another try provided she gets a job."

"Fine. Come by tomorrow with the bills, and I'll see what I can do to help."

I realized then that Agnes didn't give a rat's ass about me; she only needed someone to take over the responsibility and care for her daughter. She'd gotten the psycho bitch out of her hair and her pocketbook, and didn't want to have her back. I had a well-paying job with medical, dental and optical insurance, so I was the long-awaited answer to their prayers—the perfect guy for their beloved daughter. Now she saw the reality of what could happen; if I kicked her out, they'd be standing on her doorstep any day now.

In the end, Stacy's Mom, along with my parents, did help us get our finances back to a manageable situation. Of course, I'd later regret accepting her Mother's offer of financial assistance; it would come back to haunt me.

Things did actually improve for a month or two, once the stress of the finances had lessened; however; as I should have known, Stacy couldn't keep up the facade long before things were heading towards trouble again. Stacy's use of narcotic drugs was one of the worse problems. Her dependence on Xanax, Hydrocodone, Vicodin and Percocet were too far advanced; she'd become addicted, and I soon saw a whole new side of her emerging. She was just plain mean and hateful; there's no better way to describe it. She'd go from zero to bitch in three seconds. For a while I thought she'd forgotten my name, because I was constantly referred to as Asshole, Son-of-a-Bitch and Bastard. She began frequenting emergency rooms with any type of ailment, just to get more drugs.

By the end of the marriage, I had 42 collections on my credit report for unpaid fifty dollar co-payments. I never saw the bills when they came in the mail; they were disposed of before I got home from work. It wouldn't have really mattered anyhow; I didn't have the money to pay them. I became well known to the ER security guards and the women at the receptionist's desks. It gave me someone to talk to, but it didn't help her cause at all; the ER doctors had also become familiar with her, and stopped prescribing the medicines. I then had to drive her to other hospitals farther away. When she found an ER willing to give her the narcotics, she kept going there until they eventually caught on. Then she'd find another—and another.

Worse, Stacy would wait until Friday nights to reach the 'doctor on call' and ask them to call in her medications. If the on-call doctor refused, off to the ER we went—another fifty dollars gone.

Her Xanax addiction had escalated from 0.5 mg four times a day to 1.0 mg four times a day. However, she didn't take them as she should; she was taking seven or eight mg a day. If it was a good month, she'd make it fifteen days on a month's supply.

Something had to give.

6

They're Not Really Made
Out of Rubber

During my next therapy session, the therapist and I sat back and tried to recall everything I'd been through to date. In his eyes, I'd already undergone Control and Manipulation, Alienation of Family and Friends, Intimidation, and Substance Abuse. I had no problem agreeing with the Control and Manipulation; I readily admitted it was occurring daily, but I'd made efforts to stop some of it—especially her bedroom tactics.

He said that the alienation seemed to have been geared primarily towards my son at that point, and it appeared to be in the beginning stages with my parents. As far as friends, he said, she couldn't do much harm, since most of them were co-workers. I disagreed that she'd tried to alienate me from my son. He and I had jointly decided to limit his visits; I didn't want him around her, and he didn't want to be there. Concerning intimidation, I agreed it was in its beginning stages. It had begun with the destruction of the telephones, and had escalated to other household items.

We'd already had numerous discussions on why I couldn't break free of the hold Stacy had over me. I just couldn't put a finger on anything, really, other than the fact that if I left, I'd feel like I had failed as a husband, and I didn't handle rejection well. Also, I was terrified of being lonely again. By then, it was obvious I was becoming severely depressed. He went through the usual ritual of:

"Do you ever have any thought of harming yourself?"

44

"No; that's not an issue," I told him. "Suicide is a selfish act. Sure, it would end my pain and suffering, but what about the people who do care about me? It would harm them for the rest of their lives. So it's not an option."

"That a good outlook on it," he told me. "You're right; it *is* a selfish act. I commend you on your response . . ."

The next time I left Stacy, we were in the fourth year of our marriage. I don't remember exactly what it was that caused me to leave that time. There are many memories I've repressed over the years, and those are the ones that are haunting me now.

What I do remember is that while I was gone, Stacy got in touch with me at work while I was working the 4 to12 shift one night. She asked me to please meet her at an all-night restaurant at 12:30 AM to talk. When I arrived, she was already there and seated. It turned out she'd brought her son with her; he was 13 years old by then. Warily, I went to the table and sat down. She greeted me warmly: "Hi, Jonathan! I'm glad you decided to meet me."

"So . . . what's up?"

"Honey, I'm sorry for the things I've done. The telephones, the chairs and stuff! It's just that I run out of my medicine, and I get so crazy I don't know what I'm doing."

"Is that what you're sorry for, Stacy?" I growled. "Breaking things? How about the toll it takes on me? Doesn't that worry you?"

"But I told you, my medicine is making me do it!"

I leaned toward her. "So you feel no remorse at all about the effect it has on me; you put all the blame on the medicine. Stacy, let me put it to you bluntly: this is no one's fault but your own. You're the one abusing your medication, so what happens is your own fault. If you'd take your medicine as prescribed, maybe you wouldn't have these destructive moods. You're addicted to prescription drugs, Stacy. You need to have your psychiatrist arrange for you to get you some help!"

"Are you talking about having me committed? I'd lose my nursing license!"

"If that's what it takes, then yes, that's what I'm saying. My therapist says things will only get worse unless you admit you have a problem and get some counseling for drug addiction. And what do you need a nursing license for? You won't go to work. Your license expired two years ago anyway. You may as well face it, Stacy: you have a serious problem that's going to require professional help. You obviously can't control it on your own."

"Screw you and your therapist. I'll show both of you!" She stood up abruptly. "Let's go!" she said to her son.

I got up and followed them outside.

"Leave me alone!" Stacy screamed as I followed her out to her car. "You think I have a drug addiction? I'll show you a drug addiction!" She rooted around in her purse until she found her Xanax bottle and poured half a dozen pills into her hand, then reached into her car, got a fountain drink, and took all the pills at once. "If you hear about a car accident," she yelled at me, "don't worry. I won't be a problem to you anymore. I'll run this damn car into a tree, and I'm not scared to do it!"

Well, *I* was scared. "Stacy, you have Shawn with you; don't talk stupid shit like that! Give me your car keys and wait here while I go back inside and pay the check. Then I'll drive you home, okay?"

"Screw you, you bastard!"

I started walking back inside the restaurant, but apparently she anticipated that I was going to call the police—her instincts had always been good that way—and so she pushed her son into the car and drove off like a bat out of hell, tires squealing on the asphalt. I threw money on the countertop, gave the cashier the license number of Stacy's car and told her to call the police, then ran back to my own car. I had to speed to catch up with her, and by then she'd already reached another city district. I followed her through a series of neighborhoods until she pulled up in a police station parking lot. Her son jumped out of the car, ran to the front doors, and told the desk clerk that I was following and harassing them—and that I'd threatened to kill her.

Because society is conditioned to automatically assume the male is the bad guy in any violent situation, I was handcuffed in the parking lot and taken to a mental facility, despite my protests. No one would listen to my story. I asked them to call the neighboring police station to verify that I'd had the cashier call with Stacy's license plate number, but they didn't want to hear a word of it. To them I was simply in the denial phase of an abuser, making excuses to justify my actions. They'd seen it too many times before, sadly. At the facility, I was given a sedative to make me stop raising hell and go to sleep.

I woke up the next morning with a terrible attitude. The attendant came into my room to advise me that my breakfast tray was out on the table in the dining room. "I don't want it!" I told him.

He wasn't taking no for an answer. "You have to get up, so let's go, now."

"I said I don't want it!"

"And *I* said you have to get up; now, do you want me to call for help and forcefully remove you from this room?"

"If I get up and go get my breakfast tray, will you leave me alone?"

"Yeah, I'll leave you alone. There's a psychiatrist coming in to see you anyway."

"Okay, then, I'll get up. Remember, you said you'd leave me alone!"

I got out of the bed with nothing on but a pair of boxer shorts and walked into the dining room. There must have been 15 pairs of eyes on me, both male and female. The attendant tried to pull me back to the room to dress, but I broke free of his hold on my arm and went to an empty table, where I saw a tray of food. "Is this mine?"

"Yes, now *get back in here* and dress before you eat!"

"Okay. No problem."

I picked up the tray and looked around the room until I spotted a trash can; then I walked to the trash receptacle and threw it in as all 15 pairs of eyes watched every move I made. Then I walked back to my room, shut the door and went back to bed. A few minutes later, three attendants entered my room, dragged me out of bed, escorted me to a solitary confinement room with the padded walls, and locked me in. I'd always heard the walls in a room like this one were made of rubber, but they weren't.

I guess luck was on my side that day. About thirty minutes later, I heard a key being inserted into the door from the outside, and an attendant and a psychiatrist entered. He knew who I was, because he was Stacy's psychiatrist. (Mine was located in the same building; they were partners.) "So what's going on?" he asked, surprised. "What are you doing in here?"

I recanted the story of the previous night's episode, beginning with the call at work and ending at the police station. He looked at the attendant and said: "Put him back into his regular room; I'll take care of this."

I was escorted to my room, whereupon I sat down on the bed to wait. I wasn't sure what was going to happen next; maybe I'd get to wear the pretty white coat with the laces in the back . . . but I was surprised when the psychiatrist came back soon afterward and told me, "I have called a judge, and you are being released. I told him they had made a mistake. Your parents are coming to pick you up." When my parents did arrive and took me back to my car in the impound lot, my Mom had to pay to get it out.

The sedative they'd given me at least ensured I'd gotten a good night's sleep, so I went to work that day at 4:00.

Stacy was shocked when I answered the phone at work at 8:00 that night. She'd called the mental facility to check on me, and was told I'd been released. "How the hell did you get out?" she demanded. "I called to check on you, and they told me you'd been released. How'd you manage that?"

"Call your psychiatrist and ask him; he's the one that let me go. He said the wrong person was detained. It should have been *your* psycho ass!" I knew she'd hang up on me after that comment, and she didn't let me down.

Stacy knew that her doctor might have her committed on her next visit for prescription refills; so the next day, she called the insurance company and said she was very unhappy with her psychiatrist and requested she be reassigned to another. They agreed. As always, she'd managed to stay one step ahead of the game.

In my next therapy session, we had a discussion as to which of the abusive signs this episode fell under. "I'd say it falls under Control and Manipulation," I ventured.

"Can you explain why?"

"Because she manipulated me into following her, and then led me straight to the police station. I was a man, and they naturally assumed I was the bad guy."

He nodded. "Well, you can look at it that way. I see where you're going with that . . . but don't you think it better falls under the category of Denial? Don't you think her taking the pills put her in a position of getting caught? She shifted the blame onto you before you could tell your story, didn't she?"

He had a point. "Yes, I guess you're right; but she still manipulated me, didn't she?"

"Well . . . do you honestly think she'd have run the car into a tree with her son inside?"

" . . . No."

"Haven't you seen her take that many pills before with no adverse affects?"

"Yes."

"You knew she wouldn't run the car into the tree; it was your decision to follow her. If you hadn't, she'd have gone home."

I deflated. It was all clear to me now. "You're right," I said softly. "I made a mistake by following her. It was my fault."

"No," he said firmly. "It was *not* actively your fault; you were acting on a conditioned response. You were caught up in the moment, and worried about both her and her son's welfare. You were just a victim of circumstance. She deliberately led you to the police station, which in itself is a form of manipulation, I grant you that; but you provided her an escape from getting caught, and gave her an excuse to shift the blame. She told her son to say you'd threatened her, and you were automatically the bad guy. Even if given the chance, nothing you would have said that night about her swallowing a handful of pills would have been taken seriously."

In retrospect, you'd think I would have learned from that experience. She was punishing me for leaving home, and trying to destroy my credibility as a person. Sadly, though, it wouldn't be the last time I fell for her tricks.

Again, I don't remember exactly how I got lured back into Stacy's web. Many memories of my ordeal have been suppressed. They're lurking in the deep abyss of my subconscious, which is one of the reasons I chose to do this writing—it's therapeutic for me. Hopefully, I can force more memories to the surface, which will eventually allow me to return to work and regain my driving privileges. The incident of my boss and I having to go to personnel about the phone calls, which I discussed in a previous chapter, is a repressed memory which this writing *did* bring to the surface. That incident may be trivial to some people; however, Stacy's actions almost caused personal phone calls for everyone at work to be taken away. I couldn't carry that weight on my shoulders, and I assume it was suppressed as a defense mechanism to prevent me from going deeper into a state of depression.

My repressed memories are just one example of the evils Stacy perpetrated on my psyche. But though I'm still struggling, I survived it. Stacy might have taken away my financial stability; she might have put me through hell; she might have assaulted my dignity and self-esteem, plunged me into depression, and even stolen some of my memories. But she couldn't stifle my will to live and love, or take away my sense of humor. That's why I've tried to interject a small amount of humor into this story, especially in the chapter titles. It certainly wasn't funny when it was occurring, but to keep myself on the road for further recovery, I have to learn to accept it as the truth. Applying humor to my own misfortunes is one of my strongest healing aids.

7

She Assaulted My
Checking Account!

In my next therapy session, I was asked whether I wanted to go back with Stacy, or if I wanted to start divorce proceedings. It was difficult for me to answer, but I finally told my therapist, "I'm not sure what it is I want at this point. My head and family are pulling me one way, but my heart is pulling the other."

"So you don't want a divorce now?"

"I don't think so."

"Then what is it you *do* want?" If I'd been him, I would probably have been exasperated by this point; but he just sounded interested.

"I'd like to be happy again."

"With Stacy, you mean?"

"If I could be happy with Stacy, then yes, I'd like to try. I'm not a quitter. As long as there's hope, I won't give up."

I heard his pen scratching, and wondered what he was writing down. "Do the two of you ever go out and do things alone?"

"We go out to eat sometimes," I said. "Stacy told me she went to a nightclub with her daughter and had a good time."

"Does that bother you?"

"In a way it does. I don't like the idea of her being with another man."

"Is it because of your feelings for her, or could it be that you don't want to see her destroy another man?"

I swallowed, hard. "I do still have feelings for her, I admit that. As far as another man getting destroyed, I don't think anyone else would be stupid enough put up with it like I have."

Scratch scratch scratch. "Do you think you're stupid?"

"At this point, I don't know what I'm saying anymore." I sighed heavily. "I'm just tired of feeling this way."

"You're not stupid, Jonathan; you're just very determined to make this situation work. Why don't you ask Stacy to take you to the nightclub, and see how it goes?"

"I'm not a club person. I don't know how to dance, and I wouldn't fit in."

"Give it some thought," he suggested. "It would give the two of you a chance to be alone and have a good time together. Maybe it'll reignite a spark in your romance. You don't have to dance; just enjoy the music and go with the flow."

"I'll think about it."

The next time I talked to Stacy, I brought up the idea, and she quickly agreed it would be nice to go somewhere together. She said she'd met a woman who lived close by; they were going, and she'd meet me there. I figured she had to get there before me to shoo away all the guys she'd been flirting with.

I arrived at the designated time and walked into the place. It was a nice atmosphere, I thought. The DJ was playing disco-style music, which Stacy loved.

She saw me from the other side of the room and motioned me over to the table, then introduced me to her friend. Later, I let her talk me into a slow dance, which I didn't mind; I could do that.

As the night wore on and the beer lowered my inhibitions, I actually had a good time. Then came the awkward moment: the DJ played the song with the lyrics 'Closing Time,' and the house lights came on. I believe the song was by REM. "So, are you going back to Mommy's?" Stacy teased.

"Oh, hell, I don't know."

"You can always come home, you know."

"I just don't know if that's a good idea, Stacy. I'm confused. I don't feel anything has been resolved in our relationship."

"Oh, come on, you can sleep on the couch if you'd want. I really don't want you driving home after drinking."

I caved. "All right, all right, I guess it'll be okay."

I felt strange walking back into my own apartment after a couple weeks away. The kids appeared to be in bed, the beer had calmed me, and Stacy did look good in her dress and heels. I moved back home the next day, but with a different attitude this time. We needed more alone time like that. If I could get her away from the house and the stress, maybe she wouldn't be so angry all the time.

It worked for a while. With my rotating shift work, it was difficult; but we managed to go out as much as possible, and our relationship started recovering. She taught me a few dance moves, and I became a better and more confident dancer. I began trading off my 12-8 shifts with a guy who liked them, and I'd work his 8-4 shifts so Stacy and I could go out on weekends. We became known at the club, and made a few new friends. Everything was great for the next six months—until her insecurities got the better of her.

Every year, when tax season rolled around, I'd go to the credit union and get an income tax refund advance loan. Due to my financial situation that year, the loan officer agreed to approve the loan based on my refund; however it would be approved *only* on the condition that I allowed them to write the checks necessary to help straighten out my credit report. I didn't have a problem with that—but Stacy sure did.

Stephen, her oldest child, was getting married in two weeks, and she'd wanted to use the money for his wedding. She became irate when she learned the checks were being dispersed directly to my creditors, instead of the money being put in my pocket. Suddenly the violent tendencies increased a notch. I came home from work after the 4-12 shift one night, and found cigarette butts scattered all over the floors where she'd thrown the ashtrays around. There were dirty dishes in the sink and on the countertops, not to mention broken glasses and plates all over the place; the apartment was an absolute disaster area. She was sitting at the kitchen table chain-smoking, lying in wait for me.

She barked, "You call that credit union tomorrow and tell them they are NOT writing the checks for our bills!"

"Okay, okay, I'll call them." I was too tired to argue.

"You bring the check to me, and I'll cash it!"

That got a rise out of me. "*That's* not going to happen, Stacy!"

"And why the hell not?"

"It's a refund advance loan, Stacy. If they can't disperse the checks to pay my bills, they won't approve the loan."

"Who the hell do them people think they are, telling you how to spend your money?"

I sighed. "Stacy. They're not telling me how to spend my money; they're telling me they'll give me an advance *only* if they can put it towards the bills I owe. Otherwise, they won't give me an advance at all. If they don't, then we have to wait six or eight weeks for the refund to come by mail."

"You're a real son-of-a-bitch, you know that?"

I didn't understand the logic of that, but I rolled my eyes and said, "If you say so."

"You know the wedding's in two weeks. Now what the hell am I supposed to do?"

"Has the thought of *getting a job* ever occurred to you?"

"You're an asshole! Even if I did get a job, I wouldn't get a paycheck in time!"

"Stacy, listen closely to what I'm saying. You've known for six months this wedding was coming up. Why didn't you get a job six months ago? If you had, we wouldn't be in this situation."

She acted like I hadn't even spoken. "Did you get paid today?"

"Yes, and it went into the bank."

"Then you'll just have to give me money from your check!"

"Are you insane? Tomorrow's the fifth of the month; the rent has to be paid, or it'll be late!"

"Then *pay it late!*"

"No, I'm not paying an extra $68.00 for being late! Forget it!"

Her rage by now was incandescent. "Go screw yourself!" The boss of cola on the table was suddenly airborne. It bounced off the wall; the plastic top must not have been on tight, because on impact it came off and soda went everywhere. It was running down the walls, and had splashed back all over the table and the back of my shirt; I was standing next to the wall it hit. I don't know if she threw it at me or intentionally missed, but this was what my therapist kept warning me about. Things were getting closer and closer to being physical. "That was smart, Stacy," I told her calmly. "Now you have something to clean up."

"Screw you!"

"Not tonight, dear, I'm too tired."

"You might ever be so lucky!"

I rounded on her. "I think you need to clean this damn mess up, and hope like hell the neighbors don't file a noise complaint."

"I said screw you!"

"And I told you I was too tired. Now why don't you clean this mess up?"

I went into the bedroom, which was as disastrous as the rest of the apartment, undressed, and took a shower. I heard dishes rattling and clanging in the kitchen; *at least she's cleaning something up*, I thought. I heard the front door open and shut a couple minutes later; it opened and shut again soon after.

After I got ready for bed, I walked into the living area and saw that all the dishes in the sink and on the counter were gone. I opened the dishwasher, and it was empty.

"Where did all the dirty dishes go?" I asked Stacy.

"In the trash!" she said defiantly.

I was dumbfounded. "What, you threw them away?"

"You're damn right I did! Is there anything else you'd like me to clean up?"

"Nah, I think you've done enough for one night. I'm going to bed."

I got up the next morning and saw that Stacy had fallen asleep at the kitchen table; this wasn't an uncommon occurrence, sadly. I dressed and dropped the rent check into the slot at the apartment's office on my way to work. Much to my surprise, I didn't hear from Stacy once that day at work. However; when I came home, there was evidence she'd been shopping. Naturally, I was inquisitive. "Where did you get the money to go shopping, Stacy?"

"I withdrew it from the bank, where else?"

"How much did you take out?" I asked with concern in my voice.

"Six hundred dollars."

My jaw dropped. "Stacy, that money was for the rent! I dropped the check off this morning!"

"Oh well, I guess you better call the credit union and get them to give it back to you."

I could have strangled her. I was so irate I felt it best I leave the room. The next morning, I called the credit union and explained what had happened. They were sympathetic to my plight, but wouldn't recant their previous offer. I had no choice but to call my Mother and borrow the money for the rent. Of course, Mom was reluctant to do anything that benefited Stacy, but she put the money back into the account so the rent check could clear.

When I came home that day, I wasn't very happy to see Stacy. I was still terribly angry at that point. I went most of the evening without talking to her—and I'd later regret that decision. Looking back, I should have wondered why she didn't ask if I'd gotten the money. As it turned out, she already knew the answer, because she'd gone and withdrawn that too!

As I'd half-expected, the rent check was returned for insufficient funds. My Mom was furious, and thought I'd lost my mind for staying there. She went to the apartment complex and took a check for half of the amount due and made an agreement: they'd hold the check in good faith until I could pay the entire amount due, including the late charges, the following week. Stacy saw my Mom's car leaving the apartment complex and naturally went to inquire as to what she was doing there. One of the staff slipped and told her my Mom had paid half by check and I'd pay the full balance the next week.

Stacy was furious that my Mom had been at the complex tending to my business, and had my belongings packed and sitting by the front door when I arrived home.

Stacy had taken $1,200 out the bank and spent it on fripperies. I owed my Mother $600, and the apartment complex almost $800. Because the credit union was going to disperse the checks to pay my bills, that month's rent cost me over $2,000. Stacy was emphatic it was *not* her fault; it was the credit union's! But out of the $1,200 she took out of the bank, not one penny was spent on her son's upcoming wedding. To this day, I still have no idea where all the money went.

Needless to say, she wasn't finished with her games yet.

This next scenario she put me through caused me great remorse; even to this day, I feel sadness at its recollection. I'm blessed to have such wonderful parents who were able to see the dilemma and forgive me for my errors. I'd received a phone call from my sister at work one evening. My parents' fortieth wedding anniversary was approaching, and she wanted me to participate in preparing a celebration, to which I readily agreed.

Stacy wasn't at all pleased with the idea. "Jonathan, you don't give parties for fortieth anniversaries."

"Why not?" I asked.

"Most celebrations are given at twenty-five and fifty years!"

"Is there something that says you can't have a wedding celebration at forty years?"

"'No; it's just not traditional."

I sighed. "Well, I guess we'll be breaking tradition then; we're going to do it anyway."

"And where is your sister having this party?" she snapped.

"She rented a community building."

"Who's going to be there?"

"I don't know who's being invited, Stacy; does it really matter?"

"Yes, it does! If the parents of my ex are going to be there, then *you're* not going!"

That surprised me. Maybe she didn't want us to compare notes . . . ? "I'm sure they'll be invited," I told her, "but that doesn't mean I have to hang all over them. I mean, they're lifelong friends, and I don't think it's right not to invite them just because you don't want them there. Now, are you going with me?"

She scowled. "That's a stupid question, Jonathan. Your parents don't like me; do you really think I'd show up?"

I ground my teeth. "My parents will put their personal feelings aside for one day, Stacy; after all, it *is* a celebration, Can't you put your feelings aside and be there with me? Am I worth so little to you?"

That didn't faze her one bit. "I'm not going, Jonathan, and if the ex's parents are gonna be there, you're not going either!"

"We'll see about that!" I exclaimed. "I don't know what's wrong with you, Stacy. You've driven such a wedge between my family and me that you don't want me involved in Fourth of July cookouts, and my Mom has to juggle schedules just to keep you away from my brother and sister for Thanksgiving and Christmas. Now, those events happen every year, and I've become accustomed to it. Their fortieth anniversary, however, only occurs once, and I don't think it's fair for you try to take that away from me or my parents."

She tried a new tactic. "Jonathan, I'm not keeping you from seeing your parents on that day. You can go to the mall, buy them a gift and take it by their house before they leave to go to the party. There's nothing wrong with that, is there?"

I shrugged. "Okay, Stacy. When your daughter has her next birthday party, I get to select who can and can't attend, because I might not like them; fair enough?"

"You can't do that; she's a child!"

"Well, to my parents, I'm a child. So what's the difference?"

"You're a grown man, Jonathan," she said icily. "That's the difference."

"Then I'm *married* to a child!"

"Look. I said you're not going if them people are going to be there, and that's final!"

I called my sister and asked if "them people" were coming. She said they were invited, had responded by RSVP, and would indeed be attending. I had every intention of going. My Mom had stuck her neck out on the line to help me during the rent fiasco, and I felt it was the right thing to do; after all, they were my parents.

The party was two weeks away, and nothing had been said about it over the last week. I'd gone by a store and purchased a silver plate, arranged for it to be engraved, and told the clerk I'd pick it up the day of the anniversary. The day came, and it turned out Stacy wasn't through yet. "So are you going to the party?" she nagged.

"Yes. I told you I was."

"Fine, it's your decision. I'm just letting you know that you shouldn't come back home expecting things to be the same here."

"And what's that supposed to mean?"

"I haven't decided yet. But the minute you walk out that door to go, I'll do something. I *can* tell you when you get back all your belongings will be packed and sitting outside the door when you get home. Don't bother to knock, because I'll probably be sleeping. If you wake me up, I'll call the police and say you're harassing me."

I stared at her in disbelief. Even after all she'd put me through, I couldn't believe she was doing *this*. I finally found my voice. "You can't do that, Stacy! My name is on the lease. I live here, remember?"

She crossed her arms and looked daggers at me. "I'll tell the police we're separated, and you're bothering me."

"We're *not* separated, Stacy, that's ridiculous."

"Then I'll say all your belongings are outside the door in trash bags, but you refuse to take them. It's my word against yours! The kids will back me up! I threw you out, and you keep coming back harassing me."

I couldn't go to the complex office with the problem at hand. They were closed, and Stacy knew it. So I left and went to the mall to pick up the plate, and then went directly to my parent's house. They hadn't left yet. I explained the situation Stacy was threatening and my Mom said it was okay; they understood that I didn't need any legal problems and I should go back home. The only thing they had to say was that I really needed to think about what she was doing to me, and I should seriously consider getting out of the marriage for good.

I felt really bad on the drive back home. My heart was heavy with guilt. Why did I keep letting her do these things to me?

I pulled into the apartment complex and parked in my usual spot. As I climbed the steps to the second level, where our apartment was, I expected to see lots of bags outside the apartment door; but there were none. I used my key, went into the apartment, and saw that Stacy was asleep. Nothing had been packed. Except for the usual mess strewn about the apartment, everything appeared normal. I fixed a pot of coffee and was sitting at the kitchen table drinking a cup when Stacy walked out of the bedroom and saw me there. "I thought you were going to the party?" she grumbled.

"Stacy, just *leave me alone*! You've done enough damage for one day."

She looked confused. "I haven't done anything; I don't know what you're talking about."

"Stacy, I don't need any trouble with police just now, so leave me be. You're not my favorite person right now."

"Jonathan, do you really think I'd have done all those things I said?"

I wanted to throw the coffee in her face, but I restrained myself. "Yes, Stacy," I said evenly. "Given the crazy shit you've done in the past, I absolutely think you would have."

She looked smug. "It was all a bluff. I wanted to see if you'd make the right decision, which it appears you did. You took the gift by their house, didn't you?"

"Yes, and I told them the things you were threatening! They told me to just come back home. But it hurt them bad, I could tell, and they're blaming it *all* on you. They damn well ought to. You really screwed yourself this time, Stacy. They'll never help money-wise again, not if it benefits you in any way. They'll do anything to help *me*, but this episode pushed them to the edge as far as you're concerned. Are you happy now? The damage is irrevocable, Stacy. To them, *you do not exist!*"

When I was done, she didn't look so smug anymore.

I left her again shortly after that incident.

8

It Was a Christmas
Gift, Officer!

To be honest, I don't remember how long I stayed away from Stacy this time; in fact, I don't remember how many times I'd left by that point. Fortunately, I always had a place to go; my parents saw to that, but I'd been in and out so many times that they were really beginning to get disgusted. My father was especially fed up with my behavior and my Mom kept asking the same question: "Where did we go wrong in raising you? I just don't understand what hold she has over you."

And I kept telling her, "You didn't do anything wrong, Mom. If anything, you taught me to always try to succeed and to give it everything I have. I'm not a quitter. I know both of you are tired of me coming and going all the time."

"Is there something she's holding over your head? Something you're afraid she'll tell us? If it is, then tell us and we can talk about it!"

"No, Mom, it's nothing like that. I just can't get a grip on anything other than the fact that I don't want to be alone; I can't go through that again. Well, I guess I should rephrase it this way: I don't *want* to go through it again."

"Your Dad and I are here; you're *not* alone."

"It's just not the same, Mom. I want female companionship. You know what I mean."

"What ever happened to the girl who introduced you to Stacy?" my Mom asked. "If I could ever get a chance to talk to her face-to-face, I believe I'd have a few choice words for her!"

"I don't know. I believe she was involved in a lay-off a few years ago, and found other employment."

My Dad had given all the people in Stacy's family nicknames. Stacy's Mom was "the old bitch", Stacy was "the bitch"; the daughter was "the little bitch"; and the son was "asshole." I did find humor in that; he was right, and Stacy was raising the kids to be just like her. They had absolutely no regard for anything other than what they could get out of people—and those people should never consider getting a return on their investment. Asking to be paid back was called "harassment."

I stayed in weekly contact with the apartment complex, in order to pay the rent after Stacy's fiasco. I learned there'd been numerous complaints called in about slamming doors, constant yelling or raised voices, and what they described as someone knocking on the walls. I didn't tell the office it wasn't knocking the complainants had heard; it was household items bouncing off the walls. I'd sometimes go a whole day without contact from Stacy, and often wondered what she was doing for money. On one of my rent-paying visits, I stopped by to see if they'd torn the place up yet and soon discovered where some of their money supply was coming from.

"Stacy, where's my guitar?"

"I had to take it to a pawn shop; we needed money to eat."

To say the least, I wasn't happy. It was an expensive guitar, and it had played really well; I'd had it for years.

"How much did you get for it?"

"Two hundred dollars!"

"Give me the damn receipt. I ought to call the police; you pawned something that didn't belonging to you!"

"It's joint property. The man at the pawn shop said if you bought it while we were together, then it's half mine. Go ahead; call the police. I dare you, you bastard!"

"Give me the receipt, Stacy!" I said adamantly.

"Why, so you can take it to the police?"

"I'm going to get my guitar back. Now give me the receipt!"

"You know, you're a real son-of-a-bitch! You walk out and leave us here with no money and all you're worried about is a damn guitar!" she hissed as she handed me the pawn ticket.

"If you'd take your medicine like you're supposed to, then maybe you wouldn't be so destructive and I'd be *here*! You think it's funny to break things, but whatever you destroy will *not* be replaced!"

"Just go back to your mommy's house where there's food and someone to take care of you. I don't want you to worry about me and the kids."

There was no sense in even trying to reason with her. Her addiction had gotten farther out of control, yet she used the same excuse every time. She brought it up again when I raised the issue. "I can't go into rehabilitation because I'll lose my nursing license."

"Does it really matter, Stacy? You don't use it."

During that same time period she'd sold the washer and dryer we'd put in storage, and pawned her diamond wedding ring for $250; I'd paid over $1,500 for it. She never paid the fee to extend the contract, and it was sold.

Her venality even extended to small, petty things. For Christmas, a relative of mine had given me a pair of blue jeans for my son. Because my visits with my son were becoming few and far between, I kept his jeans in the bottom drawer of my dresser until I saw him again. It took a while for me to notice they were missing; but when I inquired, I found they'd been returned to the department store so she could buy cigarettes and fast food.

Half of the dishes and drinking glasses were missing. I was sure they'd either been broken or thrown away to keep from having to wash them.

Several days later, I went in as usual for my three-month medication visit with my psychiatrist. "So how are things going?" he asked.

"Nothing has changed, Doc. Still going back and forth."

"Are you still seeing the therapist?"

"Yes, religiously. Once a week."

"Is it benefiting you in any way?"

"Well, it helps to talk things out with an unbiased person; he sees things from a different perspective than me or my family. We're too close to the situation, I guess."

"How's your medicine working? Are you feeling any better?"

"Not really."

"Are you having suicidal thoughts?"

I lifted my head and peered at him. "Can I ask you a question, Doc?"

"Sure."

"Why do you always ask me that? I mean, if I were, do you think I'd admit it?"

He shrugged. "You'd be surprised—a lot of people do. It's their way of asking for help without coming right out and asking. They can't handle it on their own, and realize that being put into an institution is the last resort."

"Okay, I was just wondering if anyone admitted it."

"Why do you ask?" His expression was sly, calculating. "Because you think about suicide, but don't want to admit it because you're afraid you'll be put away?"

I smiled humorlessly. "Doc, I'm not going to sit here and say it's never entered my mind. Of course it has, but it's a selfish act, as I've already told the therapist—and besides, I'm a coward. I could never do anything like that."

He nodded. "So, you don't think your medication is working?"

"No, I still have bouts of deep depression. I can be sitting at work and hear a song on the radio, and I think about just going to the window and jumping. Of course I never would; I just leave the room for a while."

"Okay, I'm going to increase your Xanax to three times a day, and change your depression medicine from Paxil to Zoloft. I've seen dramatic improvements with Zoloft in other patients."

"That's fine. I don't like that Paxil. It messes with my sexual activities—when I have them, anyway."

"Okay, see me again in three months and continue to see your therapist." He started scribbling on a prescription pad—the usual illegible doctor's scrawl. "I'll send him a letter to let me know if he sees any changes in the medication switch."

"I'm sure Stacy will appreciate the increase in Xanax," I said wryly.

"You need to hide them. Do you have a locker at work?"

"Yeah, I hide money and medication at work and in my car."

"That's a good idea. Keep only a small amount of your Xanax at home, and try to keep changing your hiding place frequently. Please remember, don't take the Xanax three times a day just because the prescription says to; take them only if you feel you need to, but never take more than three a day. If you feel you need to take more, then you call me and we'll discuss it then."

Stacy had continued going to the nightclub with her girlfriend, and had started seeing a regular there. It made me jealous as hell when I found out, and much to the dismay of my parents and friends, I went running back. Everyone told me I'd lost my damned mind, and they were right. I *had* lost it. I couldn't explain the hold she had on me (I still can't), but I'd be damned if anyone else could have her!

A couple weeks later, Stacy called me at work one morning. "Did you see my car when you went out this morning?" she asked nervously.

"No, I didn't see it, but I wasn't looking for it. Why?"

"It's not there. Do you think it's been stolen?"

"Did you make the payments?"

For a second, I thought the call had been cut off. Then she finally said in a small voice: "I thought my Mom was making them."

"Well, you'd better check with her. If she didn't, it's been repossessed."

Stacy called back a few minutes later, crying. I'd been right on the money: her Mom hadn't made the payments. I called around and found that her car had indeed been repossessed. My Dad and I went to the credit union and they reluctantly gave me the loan necessary to get it back since my name was on it, but they insisted that the title be transferred to my name only—a fact which would later be to my advantage.

Stacy and I managed to limp through another month or two before we received an eviction notice for noise complaints; the office manager told me she really felt bad for me, I was a nice guy and she was extremely sorry, but rules were rules. She said they'd received over ten complaints during the time I was away and one after I'd returned. That complaint was from the neighbors next door, who obviously were not impressed with Stacy's tirades; she'd thrown a table lamp against the wall at two in the morning because I'd stayed at work an extra hour after a 4 to12 to attend a shift safety meeting. Stacy actually called my boss the next night to verify my story, and demanded I show her my check stub when I received it the next week. "There had better be one hour of overtime on it!" she said. Until she verified I was telling the truth, in her mind I was involved in another affair. Due to the declining state of my creditworthiness and money being so tight, I was at a complete loss as to where we were going to live this time.

I don't know how she did it, but Stacy conned a builder into renting us a newly-constructed house. However, as usual, the monthly rent was way above my means. I tried to argue her out of it. "Stacy, I'm sorry, but I won't sign to rent that house. I can't make the rent payments."

"Don't worry, Jonathan!" she said brightly. "I have a job interview on Tuesday!"

I remember smiling at her comment; my Dad had previously said that all her job interviews were on Tuesday. I'd never paid it much attention, but when I thought back on it, I realized he was right.

We moved into the new house, and things were actually calm for the first month; nothing was broken, and I paid all the bills and rent on time. If my memory serves me correctly, that was in early 1998. Things at the plant had begun to slow down; there wasn't much overtime, and financially it couldn't have come at a worse time. The job interview Stacy had on that Tuesday never happened; I didn't even bother to ask, since I'd grown accustomed to Stacy telling me what I wanted to hear. We'd been married for five years now, but our anniversary was treated as just another day.

I talked to the landlord often; he liked me, and knew I was doing all I could to keep us afloat, but I was getting farther and farther behind on the rent payments. Mid-year, I handed him my latest rent check and told him, "Look, I'm sorry I can't pay in full again this month."

"Mr. David, I know you're trying hard. You've been upfront and honest with me from the beginning. I know you had your reservations about signing the contract, and I remember your wife saying she'd help. I assume she isn't helping you at all, is she?"

"No sir, she's not, and I can't keep this up. I'm wearing myself down."

He looked at me speculatively. "I've decided I'm putting the house on the market soon. I'd offer you first chance at purchasing it, and I'd even consider financing for you—except that I can see no one is helping you, and I certainly don't want to put you or myself into a bad situation. It would be a no-win gamble for me to owner finance. But if you'd like to apply for a conventional mortgage on your own, I'll work with you on the down payment."

"That's very considerate of you. But you're right, it would be a struggle for me, and to be quite frank, I'd just end up losing it to foreclosure. So go ahead and list the house."

The arguments between Stacy and I increased, and she'd found a new habit: kicking holes in the bedroom doors. Three doors, to be exact. I was getting very close to what my sister had called "getting my gut full." Things got worse when I discovered her next stunt. You see, my ex-wife had gotten half of everything in my first marriage, and I soon found that she'd gotten another half of *my* half. I came home from work one afternoon and Stacy met me on the back porch.

"So how was your day?" she chirped.

"It was okay," I admitted.

"Come in this way! Anybody call you at work today?"

I couldn't understand the importance of coming in the back door, and immediately got suspicious. *What has she done this time?*

"Nobody called but you," I said cautiously. "Why, was somebody supposed to?"

"I thought you might hear from your ex-wife. I saw her today."

"Where did you see her at?"

"She came by for a while."

Something wasn't right. My ex *never* came by; she hated Stacy secondhand from all the information my son had provided her. Stacy knew my routine; I'd come in, get a glass of iced tea, then go through the den and turn right and down the hall to the bedroom to take off my safety shoes. This day, I went ahead through the back door to my bedroom, took care of my shoes, and was headed back up the hall when I noticed that something was missing: my grandfather clock. If I'd have come in the front door, I'd have noticed immediately. After glancing around the dining room, I also noticed a few other pieces of furniture were missing. "Stacy, where the hell is my clock?" I yelled.

"We needed the money, so I sold it!"

"*What?* To who?"

"Carrie; she gave me $200 for it!"

I wanted to strangle her right then and there. "What else did you sell?"

"One of the end tables by the living room sofa, and a lawnmower."

"You sold it all to my ex-wife? Dammit, Stacy, her house is half-furnished with furniture *I* paid for and now you're selling her half of what I was allowed to keep! Now she's got three-quarters of my furniture! Maybe I should move there so I can be with my belongings and my son that I never get to see!"

"Well, we didn't really need it!" she said huffily.

I knew it would be in my best interests to keep my mouth shut at this time. There wasn't much left in the house now, and if I said anything, she'd either sell or break it. "So where's the money?" I asked quietly.

"I have about $100 of it left."

I was afraid to ask the next question, because I knew I might lose my temper when I got the answer—but I had to ask. "And what did you do with the rest?

"I went and bought a few groceries and some clothes for the kids."

Later, when my temper had calmed a little, I called Carrie. She seemed quite reasonable when she realized it was me. "I was expecting a call from you," she said. "All your stuff is still on the truck. We didn't unload it yet, in case you wanted it back."

I sighed. "Why didn't you call me at work before you did this?"

"Stacy told me you were aware of it, but I didn't know whether or not to believe her. Do you want me to bring it back?"

"How much did you give her for all of it?"

"A total of $250 dollars. I paid $200 for the clock, and $50 for the end table and lawnmower."

"Well, the psycho bitch only has $100 of it left, assuming she's telling me the truth. I'll call you back."

I put down the receiver and rounded on my wife. "Stacy, give me the $100 you've got left. That clock was *not* joint property! It was my Granddad's, and I kept that because I brought it into this marriage!"

She knew she could be in trouble at this point. She went to her pocketbook, counted the money left—and found a total of $45. "I guess I spent more than I thought," she said contritely. "Are you mad because I sold it?"

That was a ridiculous question to ask me. I wasn't mad; I was infuriated! I called Carrie back. "She has $45 of it left," I told my ex. "Grass-cutting season is over. The lawnmower and end table are joint property, so keep those, but give me the option of buying my clock back. You keep it there so it doesn't get destroyed; we'll be moving soon anyway, because the bitch is allergic to work and the landlord is listing the house."

When I hung up, Stacy shouted, "I can't believe you told her I was a bitch!"

"Consider yourself lucky," I growled. "There were other words I could have used."

I guess my gut got full that day.

*   *   *

At my next therapy appointment; I was still enraged when I walked in; the therapist could see it on my face. "So what's been happening?"

"Stacy's slowly selling or breaking everything I have in the house!"

He tapped his pen on his clipboard. "What are you going to do?"

By then, I was pacing across the length of his office. "I think it's time to go for good. If I don't, I may end up in jail. I've never hit a woman before, but I came damn close that day. So close it was scary."

"Yes, it sounds like it would be a good idea to cut your losses and get out," he agreed.

The next day, I called the landlord and made arrangements to pay him all the rent he was owed, and told him I was leaving the house. I walked out a week before Christmas, during my break between the 4-12 and 12-8 shifts. I took everything I could, and went back to my parents—again. The eviction notice appeared a few days later. I'm not sure where Stacy went at first, but she and the kids ended up at her parents. I didn't see her through Christmas or New Years. Sometime in January she called and asked me to meet her at a motel; a church had put them there for a few days, because her Mother couldn't handle it anymore. She said she wanted to talk. She gave me the room number, and like a dumbass, I went there at 2:00 in the morning as she had asked.

When I knocked on the door, no one would answer. I stood there for about a minute and knocked again; still no answer. I heard someone saying something, and looked towards the front of the motel; the manager had come out and told me to get off the property. I didn't want any trouble, so I started walking back to my car—and then I had an idea. I'd drive Stacy's car home, and get someone to bring me back in the morning to pick mine up, as she didn't have a key to my car. I unlocked her car and was getting inside when I changed my mind, because I knew that if I followed through with what I intended, she'd just slash my tires or break the windows. I saw the motel manager outside again, so I got into my car and went home.

I wondered what my parents were doing awake at 3:00 am. They told me of a phone call they'd received from Stacy, and her snide remarks that I was *really* in trouble this time.

My Mom woke me up at 6:30 the next morning and said there were two policemen at the door who wanted to talk to me. I went downstairs, and they asked me to get dressed. I was handcuffed and taken away: Stacy had set me up. At the police station, I told the officers I didn't have any form of weaponry in my possession in response to a routine question—but I'd forgotten about the all-purpose knife-and-pliers tool a co-worker had given all the guys on the shift for Christmas. It was in my coat pocket, and they found it when they performed a search. I explained it had been a Christmas gift and, honestly, I'd forgotten it was in there. I knew the minute the words came out of my mouth that it sounded like something you'd hear on "C.O.P.S."; luckily, they didn't charge me with anything for having it.

I'll always remember the advice I received that day from the magistrate. Because I'd never been in trouble before, he let me go on my own recognizance. "I'm letting you out of here because you have a clean record. I was the one who took the complaint from your wife, and to be honest, I don't believe it; but if she files a report, I have to act on it, and it's up to the court system to make a determination as to whether or not her claim is valid."

"I understand, sir."

"Let me tell you this one thing: if you get in any type of trouble whatsoever, you're going to go back there." He nodded towards the door leading to the jail cells. "I can tell you won't like it back there; but there are people back there who will like *you*."

That was enough of a warning to keep me on the straight and narrow. I was allowed to read the report Stacy had filled out, and was honestly surprised that she didn't say I'd threatened to kill them all. After I'd knocked on the motel door, she'd called the office and said I was bothering her, which explains why the manager came out. She saw me going to her car—legally, it was *my* car—and called the manager again. He came back out, which is when I saw him as I drove off. Stacy was the one who called the police, and then she called my parents, waking them up. Stacy followed the police to the station, and swore out a complaint saying I was stalking her.

It was the first time I'd ever really been in trouble with the law. I had to retain a lawyer, Laura Ingram, to go with me for an arraignment the next day.

The judge set a return date for me in two weeks, after awarding Stacy a two-year restraining order. According to the order, I wasn't to be with 500 feet of Stacy or the kids. I was also ordered to complete an anger management course, which I thought was highly ironic. I wanted to speak up, but Laura nudged my side, the look on her face telling me not to say one word. The judge did allow me to use my current therapist for the anger classes. Ms. Ingram then brought up the issue of the car Stacy was driving. The honorable Judge Howard gave permission for my Dad and a third party—not me, he said, looking directly at me—to pick up the car.

Having me arrested was Stacy's way of punishing me for leaving the week before Christmas. She thought that if I filed for divorce, a criminal record would be in her favor.

After obtaining permission to pick up the car, we had someone watch Stacy's Mother's house; and when the car showed, my Dad and the third party went over there to get it. They'd called the police before they left, and arranged for an officer to meet them. According to the third party (who shall remain nameless), there were some pretty harsh words directed towards me by both Stacy and her daughter. Although I wasn't there, I got a full report on what happened, and this is how the incident played out:

They knocked on the front door after the police officer showed up; he was to do most of the initial talking. Stacy's Mom answered the door, and was told they wanted to speak to Stacy.

When she came to the door, the officer told her, "Mrs. David, I have a court order here signed by Judge Howard; I need you to give me the keys to your car, the one that's registered in your husband's name."

"Let me see that!" she said, snatching at the court order while giving my Dad a cold, hard stare. After she read the court order, she tried to be professional.

"May I have your name, Officer, to provide to my attorney?" He provided his name and badge number, both of which she wrote down. She recognized my Dad, of course, but asked the other person for his name. "I'm Third Person," he grinned.

Stacy didn't know what to think. "I need your name for my attorney, please!" she repeated.

"I told you, it's Third Person. Spelled capital T-h-i-r-d and capital P-e-r-s-o-n. See, right here on the paper: it gives permission for Mr. David, whom I'm sure you recognize as your husband's father, and a third person to pick up this automobile. I'm Third Person."

"I need to talk to my attorney!" Stacy said.

"That's fine, you have that right," the officer said. "However, you *are* going to give me the keys to the car tonight, and it *will* be returned to its rightful owner, Jonathan David. Whatever happens after tonight is none of my concern. I'm only serving you papers based on a court order signed by the judge. Now, I'm giving you ten minutes to get your personal possessions out of the car."

"I can't give you the keys tonight; my daughter's getting ready to leave and go out!"

"Not in that car she's not," the officer replied.

While they were going through the ritual of removing stuff and putting stuff in, Stacy's daughter came out to put her two cents in. "You tell that son-of-a-bitch I'll go to his house and slash his damn tires!" she spat.

"You go right ahead and do that, miss," the officer responded evenly. "But if anything at all happens to that car, ever, I'll personally come back here and arrest you—no questions asked."

Stacy knew she had no legal recourse—she was an expert at playing the legal system, after all—and handed over the keys. I'd taken Stacy completely by surprise; she wasn't expecting any retaliation from me.

I was starting to fight back.

9

A Blessing in Disguise

My therapist had been assigned to handle my court-appointed anger management classes, and here I was, going to the appointment angry; probably not the smartest move I could have made. However, he was okay once we talked a bit and I'd gotten a few things off my chest. It was completely unlike me to be angry for that long; I usually don't hold a grudge at all. I firmly believe that everyone makes mistakes and eventually feels some form of remorse after the initial feelings have worn off. But I had to keep reminding myself that I wasn't talking about most people in this case: I was talking about Stacy. She was unlike anyone I'd ever met before, and I hoped like hell I never met another woman like her.

For the life of me, I couldn't understand how she slept at night, knowing what she'd done to me. How did she deal with her conscience? Did she even have one?

These things troubled me immensely. I'd briefly mentioned during that therapy visit that if I could understand how her mind operated or even how she dealt with her actions, maybe I'd be more at ease and could come to terms with my feelings.

"That's not going to happen, Jonathan," my therapist told me bluntly. "Trying to understand her actions won't give you closure on your own issues."

"But I don't understand why she doesn't seem to feel any remorse!"

"It's bred into her personality, her upbringing. She wasn't raised in the same environment as you. In your case, you have a better sense of goodness. You were raised in a church, weren't you? "

"Yes."

"I'd be willing to say she wasn't; but that's only my professional opinion, and I may be completely wrong. She may have learned as a toddler to manipulate things to get her way. She may have thrown fits until she received what she wanted, and carried this forward with her through her prepubescent years. Somewhere along the way, she learned to punish people for not giving her what she wanted. Of course, it's hard for me to say how she operates without actually talking to her."

I sighed. "Yes, I know. It just makes me so angry that someone who says they love you can do these things."

"You've heard the old adage 'You only hurt the people you love,' haven't you?"

"Of course."

"Let's look at it this way, Jonathan; one of the reasons Stacy does these things to you is because she knows you love her in return, and therefore she puts a lot of faith in believing you won't retaliate. She knows you all too well, and she's fully aware you won't hurt her. That's one of the ways she can get away with it. I'm not saying she doesn't love you, you're just too convenient and accessible."

"That does make good sense, I guess," I admitted, after a long pause.

"Do you think Stacy would do these things to a stranger?"

"No, I don't think she would."

"Do you know *why* she wouldn't?"

"Not really."

"There's a very simple explanation," he said, tapping his pencil on his notebook. "Stacy has no way of knowing what a stranger would do in response to her tricks and games; they might very well retaliate against her. You, on the other hand, she knows very well; and no matter what she does, she knows you'll wipe it off your shoulder and keep coming back for more. When the two of you met, if you'd have been a different person, things wouldn't have turned out the way they did. If you'd had a stronger personality, she probably would have written you off immediately because she thought you wouldn't be someone she could easily control and dominate. She knows exactly what she's doing, Jonathan—and please don't take this the wrong way, but she had you marked as a target from the day you two met. She began pushing your buttons right from the start to see just how far she could push her manipulation tactics, and she's good at her craft."

I felt my heart sink, and knew that he'd hit the nail on the head. "You're damned right she's good at it! Look at me: I've been set up and arrested for stalking. I have a restraining order against me, yet here I am feeling sorry for her because I don't think she understands what she's doing."

He snorted. "Jonathan, you've got to get that idea out of your head; she knows *exactly* what she's doing. Don't fool yourself. She's been doing it her whole life, and she's perfected the art. Again, I'm sorry to have to tell you these things—but it's the way Stacy lives. She's a survivor."

"But I feel like such a damn fool. I was so stupid for going there that night; I should have known better!"

"Yes, you probably knew you shouldn't, but it's built into your nature. You're the type who always looks for the good in everyone. You're a trusting guy—maybe even too trusting. There's absolutely nothing wrong with possessing those qualities; they're great virtues to have, but please understand, you're not the only one possessing these traits. There are many, many good men just like you out in the world. However, there are also many Stacy's out there, and their purpose in life is to seek out and prey upon these men. It doesn't take them long to recognize their targets and start their games."

"That's a terrible way to live, taking advantage of people like me. So she probably never did love me?"

To my surprise, my therapist said, "No, I'm sure she does, in her own way. She appreciates the qualities you possess, but she also capitalizes on them for her own personal gain. Think of Stacy as having a fish on the hook. She catches you and takes everything she can until there's nothing left; then either you've had enough and walk away or she releases you back into the water. People like Stacy will eat honest and good-hearted people like you for breakfast, and not lose a minute of sleep over it as long as they're satisfied with the results. There's no need to waste time blaming yourself. It's what you have inside of you that knows the truth, and that's all that matters."

I couldn't let it go. "But what about other people? Since the stalking arrest, I feel like people look at me like I'm some kind of freak who goes creeping around in the middle of the night preying on women!"

"Jonathan, the only thing that matters right now is what you think of yourself, and what your family and friends think of you. They know you better than that, and they don't see you as some kind of sexual deviant. The only people who would are the people Stacy has gotten to, and their opinions should be the last of your worries right now."

"I just feel like such a damn fool. I fell for one of the classic examples of Control and Manipulation. She threw the bait in the water and I took it, hook, line and sinker. I did exactly what she wanted me to do."

"Maybe this is what it took to make you be more cautious from now on. She put you in a situation involving the law this time, with much more serious consequences than before. Hopefully you've learned from your misfortunes."

"I'm worried to death about going to court," I admitted. "What if she's successful? She's a damned good actress!"

"Don't worry about it. You have a good attorney—I've seen Ms. Ingram in action. She's no pushover, and she has a very high success rate in matters such as yours. In fact, she has a real problem with women who take advantage of unsuspecting men."

"That's kind of the opposite of what I'd expect of a woman attorney," I admitted. "You'd think she'd be on the side of the woman."

He shrugged. "I suppose she's opposite of the stereotypical woman lawyer, and I have no idea why. Be that as it may, taking on manipulative women is her forte. You're in good hands, Jonathan. Now let's change the subject for a few minutes. There's one thing you do quite often, and you really need to work on it. You ruminate."

That was a word I hadn't heard before. "What's that mean?"

"Well, you think too much. You create scenarios in your head, and you act on them. I'd bet inside your head, you're always playing the 'what if' game. 'What if she wins? What if this or that happens?' You'll drive yourself insane if you keep it up. Well . . . I don't actually mean you'll literally go insane, but you'll always be in constant turmoil over something that hasn't happened, and may never happen."

"I can't help it. I've always done that." I smiled a little. "I'm already insane, anyway."

"And why do you say that?"

"I read somewhere that the definition of insanity is repeating the same behavior over and over again, but expecting a different result every time. Isn't that what I do with Stacy? I leave and go back, thinking things are going to get better or things are going to be different—yet they never are."

He looked at me speculatively. "Yes, I've heard that, and to an extent it's true; however, you're not insane. You've just been the victim of a scheming woman. You never saw it coming, Jonathan, because that's the way you are. If you were really insane, you wouldn't be able to differentiate between sanity and insanity at all."

"Huh. Yeah, I've heard that too."

"Jonathan, please keep this in mind: the best predictor of the future is the past." He leaned toward me and looked me in the eye. "History repeats itself. People rarely change, and if they do, it's only temporary. Sooner or later the real person is going to re-emerge. Let's look at Stacy as an example; she's an actress, you said, so think about the past. Hasn't she always given you the impression she's changed and learned from her mistakes, and lured you back into her 'web' as you call it?"

"Yes . . . every time but once, the time she made me jealous and I went running back."

"During those times, did she really change or was it only an act?"

"It was an act," I admitted.

He leaned back and nodded. "And it'll always be an act. Making you jealous was *also* a game to her. She more than likely planned the whole thing, and used another unsuspecting male to achieve her goal. She led him on only as a ruse to get you back. I'd be willing to bet she didn't play any games with him other than acting as if she was interested; but it worked, didn't it?"

"Yes, it did," I said softly.

"Stacy is like a chameleon, Jonathan. She can change her appearance to fit her games and avoid being captured—but in reality, no matter which appearance or face she's using at the time, she's still a chameleon."

"I'd still prefer to think of her as a black widow spider, constantly luring me back into her web of deceit. I just have to detour through hell to get there."

He shook his head sadly. "Jonathan, you've got to learn to take one day at a time; live in the present! The past is gone; you can't change what's happened, so just try to learn from your mistakes. You can't predict the future, but you're still always trying with the 'what if' games."

"Well, nine of out ten times I guess right," I grumbled.

"Okay, then, how does this make you feel? This incident with you going to the motel is the one time out of the ten you were wrong, wasn't it?"

"But if the past is the best indicator of the future, aren't my 'what if' games somewhat justified? What if she tries *this* again; or what if she tries *that*?"

"I see your point, but there's an easy answer to this: DON'T do the things you did in the past. That's lesson one. Lesson two: there's always a scheme developing in her head. If Plan A doesn't work, she'll switch to Plan B. You should know all her games by now. Don't act on them! Take control of your actions; *you* are the one responsible. Remember that she's also thinking about the past; her tricks worked before, and she's sure they'll work again. You have to live for today. Beat her at her own game."

"I understand. So what are we supposed to do for anger management?"

He grinned. "We're doing it now. I'm trying to make you live for today, the present. The past makes you angry. Stop rehashing it in your head. Stop living there and playing the ruminating game, and the anger—and probably the traps you keep falling into—will go away."

"I'll try," I said dubiously.

"Do try, Jonathan. You're a very complex person, a deep thinker. Your mind never stops. You're always delving deep into something that's unnecessary for you to worry about. I know you've probably been that way for quite a while, but you need to learn to relax a little bit. When you play the 'what if' game, you've cooked and eaten a fish you haven't even caught yet. Live in the now, Jonathan; be more careful of your present activities, and the past won't come back to haunt you.

"I'll do my best."

"Now, knowing you like I do, you're going to get this hare-brained scheme into your head that you have to talk to her; it's eating you up inside to find out why she did it. DON'T DO IT! Don't have any friends or family attempt to contact Stacy to get the answers. If you feel you have to talk to someone, call my answering service and leave a message. They'll get in touch with me, and I'll call you. Promise me you'll do that, Jonathan."

"I don't think I have to worry about that," I said earnestly. "The magistrate put the fear of God in me that day. I don't want to meet Bubba!"

"Good. Now go to work and do your job. Get together with your friends. Didn't you tell me once you played guitars with one of your co-workers? See if he's interested in doing it again. Find a way to occupy your time, and keep from ruminating. You'll get through this."

On the drive home, I thought about some of the things I'd learned. I'd never thought about things the way he put them; but I realized that he was right, now that I'd given it some thought. The past really was a good predictor of the future. I'd always heard the saying that 'history repeats itself.' He also saw right through me; it was driving me crazy, I *did* want to talk to Stacy to find out why she'd done it to me, but the magistrate's words kept me from picking up the phone and calling her Mom's house. All it would take was one foolish mistake, and I'd be Bubba's bitch until April, when the case went to trial. I certainly hoped I didn't have a weak moment and mess up.

My restraining order specifically said that I had to keep at least 500 feet away from Stacy and the kids. I'd asked the therapist what I should do if I was sitting in a restaurant having dinner with my parents—or anyone, for that matter—and Stacy came in. His instructions were to get up and leave, which was completely unfair in my eyes. How did I know she wouldn't watch me, and play games to continue her manipulation tactics? Why should I have to suffer if I was there first? It all boiled down to the fact that Stacy had gotten the law involved first, and had the advantage.

My parents came up with another possible scenario one evening, along the same lines, and I'm certainly glad they did. Even with my incessant ruminating, as my therapist put it, I hadn't thought of it before—and neither had my therapist. Stacy might still be on a revenge streak because I'd taken the car away, and might try to set me up again. It was at their suggestion that I arranged for a co-worker to take me to and from work as often as possible. As they pointed out, it wouldn't be out of character for Stacy to get ahead of me while driving on the highway and then slam on the brakes, causing me to rear-end the car she was in. Since it was a rear-end collision, I'd immediately be at fault, and Stacy would say I was continuing my stalking and had done it deliberately. I'd be in violation of my restraining order, and I'd spend the remaining time until court in jail with Bubba.

After talking to Ms. Ingram about this and other issues, she suggested I begin keeping a daily journal of my activities, tracking things such as what time I went to work, what time I came home, who I talked to on the phone, what TV shows I watched, etc. "You never know if Stacy may try to pull something, and if you have some type of alibi, it will definitely be in your favor," she told me.

"I understand. But what if she says I was following her around the mall or something? Isn't it going to come down to my word against hers? Who are they going to believe?"

"Yes, and what if you were talking to your brother or sister on the phone at that time, and your phone records prove it?" she pointed out. "See what I mean? Having *something* to substantiate your claim is better than nothing at all. Never go into a public place alone, especially one where you know it's a possibility you could run into her, like the mall or Wal-Mart. Always have someone with you as a witness on your behalf. You can never be too careful, Jonathan. I've been through similar situations with other clients like this, but I have to admit, none have been as devious as Stacy. I'm only trying to help you, okay?"

I dove into my work at full speed. I started working all the available overtime I could, since I had to raise money for my rapidly-climbing legal fees. I had a problem with my off days; I needed something to do, so I decided to call Cynthia, a woman I'd briefly dated before I'd ever met Stacy. We spent some time together, and had good times.

I was progressing nicely through the healing process; Stacy was on my mind less and less with each passing day. I'm not saying there weren't bad days; driving by places we'd been together during our good times was sometimes tough, but I'd learned to quickly focus my attention to something else. The occasional song on the car radio was an easy fix: change the station. If at work, it would be rude to get up and change the radio station, so I simply left the room; I found the best treatment was to go to the restroom or take a walk.

It had been almost two weeks since the stalking incident; I don't remember if I was working 4-12 or had worked over onto it, but I answered the phone and heard the voice of Stacy's Mom. "Jonathan! What the hell is wrong with you, stalking Stacy like that?"

I rolled my eyes. "I wasn't stalking her," I said resolutely. "She told me to come there. She set me up because I left the house the week before Christmas."

"Oh, bullshit! I don't believe that!"

"Well, whatever. It'll all come out in court."

"Listen, I want to make a deal with you. If you let Stacy have the car back, I'll make the payments."

"Nope, no way."

She raised her voice, the harpy. "Look, her and them kids of hers are getting on my last nerve! I need a way to get them out of my house. That car's not doing anything but sitting in your driveway, and you're making the payments!"

I said patiently, "I have a restraining order issued against me that says I can't be within 500 feet of Stacy or the kids."

"You don't have to bring it here; I'll get Stacy's Dad to bring me over to your house and pick it up. That way, you won't be doing anything wrong."

"What I'm trying to say is, I can't be within 500 feet of any of them, and I'm sure she's standing right there listening to everything you say," I responded. "As far as I know, she could be on another extension listening to both of us; this phone call was probably her idea anyway. I have witnesses here at work who will verify that I'm telling you these things right now. If you want to make car payments, the best advice I can give you is to go out and buy her a car; she's not getting the car back from me. I'd give it away before I'd let her have it. She's the one responsible for this situation, not me. If you don't want them in your house, then put 'em out on the street. Stacy is a survivor; she'll be okay."

"Why are you being so mean to me, Jonathan? I'm an old lady!"

"I'm not being mean at all, Agnes. I'm only stating the facts. Stacy set me up; she had me arrested for stalking, and she doesn't give a shit what she's done to me. Neither would you, except now *you're* inconvenienced! I'm sorry, but I'm not letting her have the car back. She should have thought things through before she had me arrested on stalking charges. She never considered the consequences her actions would have on you. Her only concern was a burning revenge towards me, and she got what she wanted. That car just happened to be an ace I had up my sleeve, and I played it fair and square. Now, I'm not allowed to call your home because Stacy is living there, so I'd greatly appreciate it if you'd reciprocate and not call my home or my employer. I've written down a record of this call and I will so advise my lawyer; I do have witnesses. Goodbye."

I was very surprised at my responses; I don't know where they came from, but I liked it! My coworkers were also impressed. They'd begun to see a trace of the person I was before Stacy. My job performance was improving; I was beginning to feel relieved, as if a giant weight had been lifted from my shoulders. I had previously been worried about my off days, wondering how I'd spend the time. Now they couldn't get here fast enough, and there weren't enough of them. I'd worked more than enough to pay my legal fees, had my bills under control, and was also helping out my parents. I hadn't been this happy in a long time. That's not to say I didn't have my bad moments; there were times when the memories would creep in and I'd feel sad for the way I'd talked to Stacy's Mom; it wasn't my nature to be disrespectful. But hadn't she started the conversation off on the wrong foot by accusing me of stalking her daughter?

I'd spent quite a few weekends at my sister's house, which was an hour away from my parents' in the opposite direction from Stacy. On one of those weekends, I'd gotten her to take me to a car dealership where she and her husband had always bought their vehicles. I saw a new 1999 Pontiac Firebird there that I just had to have! I decided to go to my credit union and see what they'd say. I was fully expecting to hear, "I'm sorry, not at this time." I sat down with the loan officer and explained what had happened. When I told her I had a restraining order and couldn't be around Stacy for two years, I could see her relax a little. She'd known me for years. I'd been dealing with them since I began my employment, and I'd never been late on a payment. She never actually said it, but I felt Stacy was one of the reason's they'd been reluctant to loan me money lately. I told her about the car and that I'd already negotiated a good deal. "I'll be trading in both cars," I pointed out, "the Firebird and Stacy's car. I just recently took out a loan to get hers out of repossession. Both loans would be paid off. The car I want to buy is only a couple thousand more than those two combined, but the payment is lower."

She referred me to the Vice President's office, and I again explained my situation. The VP seemed to be very pleased about the restraining order keeping me away from Stacy. I explained that my finances were under control, even though my credit score had not jumped dramatically. However, when she pulled my credit, she saw I was definitely making headway as far as making arrangements with the forty-two collection accounts, and my bills were beginning to show that I was paying on time. She saw that I was well on the way to improving my creditworthiness. She'd always valued my honesty and my willingness to be up front about everything. She asked to see the paperwork on the new Firebird, and called the dealership to verify the figures. I walked out within an hour's time with a check to cover the difference between the two trades and the new car. I made arrangements with my Dad to drive one of the cars, and told the dealership I'd be there within two hours.

Later I drove the new car home.

Having Stacy out of my life was definitely beginning to have positive effects; I was much happier, feeling much better, and realized that I hadn't lost the reputation I thought I'd never see again. I hadn't had the car 24 hours when I received a phone call at work from Stacy's Mom.

"Jonathan, I like your new car! It's pretty! When did you get it?"

"Why don't you tell me? You're the one keeping tabs."

"You should be ashamed of yourself, buying a new car while your wife is over here with them kids eating all my food and driving me crazy."

"Talk to your daughter about why she's there. We've already had this conversation once, remember?"

"Well, you just remember," she said unhappily, "I helped you pay some of your bills!"

I snorted. "I'm sorry, but there seems to be a misunderstanding. The bills you helped pay were not for *my* benefit, but for the benefit of your daughter and grandkids. I could pay *my* bills; it was her spending habits that I couldn't afford, and she wouldn't lift a finger to help—so the way I see it, it was her expenditures that you gave me money for. Not one penny of that money was for my benefit. It was your idea to help me with the finances if I went back; you offered, I didn't ask. Don't try to hold that issue over my head. Please, don't call me at work anymore or I'll notify my attorney, and she can have a restraining order taken out on you for stalking and harassment at my workplace."

"How you gonna get me for that?"

"I told you last time you called not to bother me at work or home. I've had my new car less than 24 hours; it was dark when I brought it home, and I left for work this morning at 6:45. So it's obvious that someone's staking out my parents' home. You were the one to call and inquire about it, and it was also you that said it was a pretty car; how could you have come to that determination if you hadn't been riding by my parent's home to see it? If I relay this information to my lawyer, she'll assume it's you who came by at night and noticed; ergo, you are stalking."

"That's ridiculous!"

"Sure it is, but until you go to court and prove otherwise, you'll be labeled as a stalker—and you'll have to pay out a lot of money in legal fees to prove your innocence."

"I don't have that kind of money, and you know it!"

"Well, now we're getting somewhere. I don't have it either, but your daughter filed false accusations against me, and I have to spend money I don't have to prove my innocence. So what makes you so special that you can't do the same? Welcome to Stacy's world! Goodbye!"

Things were finally beginning to look up. I was holding my ground with Stacy's Mom, and playing the games she'd taught Stacy so well. Her Mom was getting a feel of what it was like to be intimidated.

10

Court is in Session

From the time I bought the new car until my court date in April, I had some of the best times I could remember since I'd met Stacy and my life began its downward spiral. I'd begun spending more time with Cynthia.

It was always a joy to go out in public with Cynthia; she was a very nice-looking woman. She always turned heads when entering a room; but as the saying goes, "Every rose has its thorn." It didn't take long for me to realize that she wasn't the type of woman I'd want to settle down with; she had more than her fair share of phobias and unusual characteristics, and I certainly didn't want to jump back into the frying pan. But we got along well and always had a good time together.

Because of her past failed marriages, she'd developed a fear of relationships. I was okay with this; in fact, I was ecstatic about it. I wasn't looking to jump into another marriage. We'd only had sexual relations a couple of times; we preferred to be friends who were helping each other get through bad times in our lives.

Neither I nor Stacy had begun divorce proceedings at that point. I'd been advised by my lawyer to wait until the court date for the stalking charges was finalized. "After the court date, you'll have a much better chance of obtaining an uncontested divorce," Ms. Ingram pointed out.

"If things go in my favor, right?"

"That's not even a question, Jonathan. Things *will* go in your favor."

"How can you be so sure of that?"

"Jonathan, you're paying me good money to do my job. I've done my homework. I have enough information on Stacy that you don't need to worry about the stalking charges."

I grinned. "Good! I just want it to be over so I can continue with my life. I want all this behind me."

My work performance was great, I hadn't lost the respect of my co-workers, and I had a social life again. After my court appearance was over, it would be sunny days and clear blue skies ahead. I didn't see any obstacles in my way—that is, I didn't until the doorbell rang one morning, and I saw an employee of the Sheriff's department standing on the porch. "Are you Jonathan David?" the deputy asked.

"Yes, I am."

"You have been served," he said, and handed me a piece of paper.

Stacy's Mother must not have appreciated my attitude with her those two times on the phone. She'd taken out a Warrant in Debt against me for the money she'd given me to help get the bills under control if only I'd go back with Stacy. I was furious that she'd gone to such lengths. I called my lawyer immediately, and set up an appointment for the next day. "Can you believe this shit?" I said when I stormed into her office. "They just don't ever stop!"

"Don't worry about it," she advised calmly.

"But this court date is *before* the stalking date!"

"Jonathan, let me worry about this. I'll have this case continued until after the stalking case is over."

"But if I lose in court, it'll only be worse, won't it?"

She looked at me severely. "Jonathan, do you remember me telling you that I've done my homework?"

"Yes."

"Then let me handle this, okay?"

"Fine," I said grudgingly.

When I went to my next weekly visit with my therapist, I was able to vent some of my frustrations. "So how are things going?" he asked.

"You won't believe it," I growled. "Just when I can see the light at the end of the tunnel, Stacy's Mom takes out a Warrant in Debt for the money she gave me that time to help pay the bills if I'd agree to go back to Stacy."

"Did you sign anything with her?"

"No, it was more for Stacy's benefit than mine. She's a conniving bitch."

The therapist pursed his lips in thought. "Well, I'm not sure of all the legal ramifications, but it seems that since the two of you are still married, Stacy should be responsible for half of it. Have you talked to Ms. Ingram about it?"

"Yes. She'll take care of it. She said she'll have it continued until after the stalking trial; let the old lady wait a little while."

"Well, there you go. Let Ms. Ingram handle it, Jonathan. No sense worrying about it. Now: everything else okay with you?"

"Yes, I'm doing good, and I'm feeling a lot better."

"Great! Well, it won't be long before your trial date will be past."

"Yeah. I just hope you don't have to come to jail to continue our sessions."

"Don't be ridiculous; you're not going to jail. The very worst thing that could happen would be that you'd get probation, and the restraining order would still be in effect."

"I hope you're right."

"When do you see your lawyer again?"

"The Monday before court."

"Give her this when you go." He handed me an envelope addressed to the attorney and Judge Howard.

I looked it over dubiously. "What is it?"

"The results of your anger management course. You can read it if you like."

I opened the envelope, fully expecting to read a note revealing that I'd been set up by a ruthless, cold-blooded snake; however, as usual, I was wrong. In fact, I missed this one by a long shot, and I wasn't happy at all—as he could see by the expression on my face after I'd finished reading the report. "This isn't true!" I blurted.

"Why not?"

"It's just not the way it is."

"So read it out loud to me and we'll talk about it."

"Okay, but I still don't like it." The letter stated:

Honorable Judge Howard and Ms. Laura Ingram, Attorney at Law

> *I have counseled Mr. David for his court-appointed Anger Management Classes. Mr. David faithfully attended every session and was very cooperative and insightful. Mr. David is fully aware of the mistakes he made leading up to this event, and he feels great remorse for his actions. Mr. David has duly stated that he has learned from his mistakes and will no longer act in this manner and wishes the court to take this matter into consideration for his upcoming trial.*
>
> *Respectfully yours . . . .*

"Now: what's wrong with it?" the therapist asked.

"It's not true! I didn't do anything wrong! I was set up!"

"Jonathan, let me explain a few things to you. All that information will come out in the court trial if it needs to, and the judge will hear it then. My purpose was to make you see the error of your ways, especially in going to the motel that night. The letter doesn't say you're guilty; it just says you didn't use your best judgment when you went to the motel. If the opportunity presented itself again, would you go meet Stacy?"

"Hell no."

"Why not?"

"Because it was a stupid thing to do!"

"That's what the letter is saying. You realized you made mistakes, and won't do them again."

"Well, it sure doesn't sound that way."

"Believe me, I've written many of these, and it's what the judge wants to see."

I met with my attorney the day before court. "Have you heard anything from Stacy's lawyer?" I asked her.

"Not a word. I honestly don't believe she has one, and I'd be willing to bet she doesn't even show up for court."

"Just curious . . . I have the same feeling, but why do *you* think that?"

"Just my gut feeling." Ms. Ingram smiled grimly. "In my opinion, Stacy acts on impulse and does things without thinking them through. After some time has passed and she realizes what she's done, she drops it. I bet she's never carried any project through to completion, has she?"

"Yes, I know of one," I said.

"What was that?"

"She conned me into marrying her," I said grimly.

"Okay, I'll give you that one. Now, I need to give you some advice before we go into the courtroom tomorrow. First of all, and this is important, don't speak unless spoken to, okay?"

"I understand that. I've read a lot of legal thrillers. You open your mouth and you open a door for the other attorney to jump into."

"Good, you're aware of that. If you let me do my job and do all the talking, things will be fine. If you're asked a question, you look at me and I'll let you know whether to answer it or not. Now go home, relax, get a good night's rest and I'll see you at court in the morning."

It wasn't as easy as Ms. Ingram made it out to be; I had a very hard time sleeping that night. I kept thinking back to the words of the magistrate, and wondered if it would be the last night I slept in my own bed for a while. I didn't want to sleep with one eye open next to Bubba and his other bitches.

I'm not sure when I fell asleep, but the next morning seemed to come quickly—and I was a nervous wreck. I put on a suit and tie and anxiously went to court with my parents. I'd asked Ms. Ingram if I could bring Cynthia along, but she said it wouldn't be a good idea to flaunt another woman in front of Stacy in a court of law, since we hadn't started divorce proceedings. She had a very good point there.

We stood in the vestibule outside the courtroom, watching both the traffic and the clock; Ms. Ingram hadn't shown up yet, but neither had Stacy. I felt a rush of relief when I saw Ms. Ingram exit a car and head towards the courthouse; she waltzed into the front doors of the building like she had not a single care in the world. "Everybody ready?" she asked breezily.

"Let's just get this over with," I said, tugging at my collar.

"Is Stacy already inside?" she asked.

"Haven't seen her yet."

"She's not going to show up, just like I predicted." She glanced at her watch. "Well, it's just about show time. Let's go inside the courtroom."

When we walked in, there was nobody else inside at all. Eventually the bailiff came in behind us, closed the doors, and walked to the front before disappearing through a door behind the judge's bench.

Still no Stacy.

"All rise for the Honorable Judge Howard," the bailiff said, as he re-entered the courtroom. We all stood, and the judge I'd seen too many times came out and took his seat on the bench. "This is the case of Stacy David, plaintiff, vs. Jonathan David, defendant," the bailiff announced.

The judge flipped through a file, then looked at me owlishly. "Mr. David, you're accused of stalking your wife?" Judge Howard asked.

"That's correct, Your Honor," Ms. Ingram replied snappily.

"Is anyone here representing Mrs. David in this matter?" Judge Howard asked.

Looking around the courtroom, I saw that the only people present were myself, my attorney, my parents, the bailiff and the judge.

"Your Honor," Ms. Ingram said, "It would appear that Mrs. David hasn't bothered to show up. I feel that if Mrs. David can't bother to attend court to defend her charges and accusations against my client, the court should take this into account and dismiss all charges against my client. My client has attended anger management classes as ordered by Your Honor, and has done exactly as instructed. He has had no contact at all with Mrs. David." She handed the paper to the bailiff, who then handed it to the judge. He quickly perused the report.

"This report complies with the court," the honorable judge said. "Mrs. Ingram, as far as dismissing the charges goes, I'm inclined to agree. If Mrs. David can't be bothered to show up to defend the charges she filed, I'm ruling in favor of your client. This case is dismissed. However, Mr. David, the restraining order is still in effect."

"My client is aware of that fact, Your Honor. Thank you."

I felt as if another great weight had been lifted from my shoulders. I wouldn't have a criminal record after all! Life was good!

We all stood outside the courtroom talking for a few minutes. Next on the agenda was the Warrant in Debt from Stacy's Mom. I knew without a doubt *she* would show up for court, as money-hungry as she was. After all, someone had to replace all the blood that Stacy and the kids had drained from her; and who better than me? I had a job!

"So what about your divorce; are you ready to start the paperwork yet?" Ms. Ingram asked.

"I'd like to wait until after this Warrant in Debt case is over. If I file for divorce now, she'll just have that much more in for me when we go to court."

"Your choice, Jonathan. But you *are* going to file, right?"

I said reluctantly, "I know it has to be done. It just makes me sad to think about divorce. I don't want to go through another one."

"Well, this one should be one hell of a lot easier than the last."

"I sure hope so."

Over the next month, I'd occasionally see Stacy's kids out on the streets in cars or at the mall. I couldn't help it if I unknowingly passed them on the road; however, I hadn't seen Stacy since the arraignment back in January. She was either sucking the blood out of someone else by now, or holed up in bed taking medicines all day as usual.

There had been numerous occasions where I'd pull up at a stoplight and someone next to me would blow the horn. I'd look in the direction of the horn and see Shawn, Stacy's youngest, flipping me the finger. I'd write down the license plate numbers of the vehicles and advise my lawyer, but her advice was to ignore it. It wasn't worth the time or money to pursue it.

The whole stalking fiasco Stacy had initiated cost me countless hours of lost sleep, not to mention productive time lost to worry and depression. I'd paid out over $3,000 in legal fees and had probably lost another $2,000 in wages because I had to attend arraignments, court dates and weekly therapy sessions. You can imagine my anger when Stacy never bothered to show up; it was all for nothing.

Looking back, I guess I should have felt fortunate that the judge kept the restraining order in place, or I'd have probably gotten myself in trouble again. Or at least, in trouble a lot sooner than I was going to anyway.

I guess I'll never learn.

11

Caramel Praline Crunch

Overall, I'd been enjoying my life since I'd put Stacy behind me. I'd graduated from the school of therapy and was sent back out into the real world—but I soon found out I wasn't ready to be on my own quite yet. I was still vulnerable, and had some valuable lessons to learn. I was still seeing Cynthia; we went out often. I also dated a few other women, but nothing seemed to click between us. It didn't matter which direction I went, I'd always find myself back at the same place: Lonelyheartsville. I kept myself busy with my job, and worked a lot of overtime. I'd been actively working with debt collectors to repair the damage Stacy had done to my credit; it was a long and tedious process, but I was definitely making some headway. There were forty-two collection accounts from ER visits at fifty dollars apiece, and I knew it wouldn't be an overnight fix; in fact, it would take 7-10 years for all of them to disappear from my credit reports. However, I took solace in knowing that a satisfied collection showed progress and determination, at least on my part, though it would be a while before creditors saw my diligent efforts.

One afternoon I ran into the nymphomaniac, the one I was dating before I met Stacy. We agreed to get together that night and go hear a band play at a popular Thursday night party spot that opened every spring and ran throughout most of the summer. I made it clear before we went out I wasn't interested in sex; I'd begun to associate sex with trouble, thanks to Stacy.

We went to hear the band and had a decent time, and I took her home. Even though I'd already stated that sex wasn't on my mind, it was definitely on hers—and I knew she was going to try and change mine. It had been an enjoyable evening, and somehow I actually got away without having to go inside her home. Looking back now, I realize I should have let her have her way with me. I had no idea what was waiting for me just around the corner.

I was driving home that night when fate intervened and started the whole nightmare process over again. My parents had been buying a new type of ice cream called Caramel Praline Crunch, and I just plain loved it. I'd finished up the last of it at home the night before, so I decided to stop at Wal-Mart to buy some on my way home.

As I was exiting my car in the parking lot, I heard someone calling my name.

I turned to look toward the direction of the voice. It was Stacy's son, Shawn, the one who found it so amusing to flip me off every time he passed me on the road. I started to walk towards the store when he spoke again. "Are you too good to speak?"

I turned in his direction and said, "You know I'm not supposed to be within 500 feet of you, or make any attempts to contact you." I turned back toward my car to leave. I certainly didn't want any trouble, and I thought it would be best if I just forgot about the ice cream. It wasn't important enough to risk going to jail over.

"Hey, man, you didn't contact me, I spoke to you. It's cool, man. All that stuff is over with anyhow. Nice car! When did you get it?"

"I don't know . . ." I said slowly. "Something doesn't feel right. I think I should just leave."

"Nah, I said it's cool, man! We're just hangin' here."

"I have to go," I insisted.

"Oh, hey, go on into the store and get what you needed. You don't have to leave—I won't say anything. Everything's cool, man!"

I've always heard that whether it's innocent baby birds or venomous snakes, when you see one of their offspring, you can rest assured the mother is nearby. I knew this to be true and knew I should leave; however; I had a weak moment. Was I subconsciously hoping to encounter the Black Widow, even though my senses were telling me to go? I could feel the urge, the power pulling me to the store, and was unable to resist the attraction. Hell, maybe it was the Caramel Praline Crunch calling out to me.

I'd gotten the half-gallon of ice cream from the freezer and was walking back toward the main aisle when the she-devil herself turned into the aisle and stood right in front of me, her hands gripping a shopping cart. My fears emerged, and without saying a word, I walked around her cart and was ready to make the turn towards the registers when I heard: "Jonny!"

I stopped dead in my tracks. I was scared as hell to turn around. I didn't know what to do. My gut instinct was telling me, *Go; walk to the registers, run, as fast as you can, get away!* But my feet wouldn't move. I heard it again: "Jonny, don't go."

I did what I felt was best; I conquered the force drawing me to her, and walked away. I went to the checkout, paid, and then looked in all directions before I headed towards the doors. There was no sign of Stacy until I turned the corner to get to the exit and she was there, waiting for me.

"Please don't go. I want to talk to you," she said sweetly.

"Um, I have a restraining order against me, Stacy. You know I can't talk to you; I'll go to jail. Sorry!"

She rolled her eyes. "Jonathan, that's over with!"

"Not according to the judge it's not."

She snorted. "I'm not going to tell anyone. I'll go to the judge and have it lifted. So . . . how'd your court date go?"

Luckily one of the security guards had taken position nearby, and I spoke loud enough for him to hear. "Stacy, I have a restraining order against me that says I'm not supposed to talk to you. I'm sorry. Leave me alone."

"Jonathan, I told you I'll have it lifted. It's not a problem. I won't say a word, I promise!"

I looked at the security guard as if he were going to give me instructions; I needed someone to tell me what to do. If he would have just nodded his head towards the doors, I would have run; but he just watched as I stood there looking for an answer. The force was pulling me again. I shrugged. "Okay, he's my witness. What do you want?"

"How'd your court case go?"

"It was dismissed because you didn't show up."

She smiled brightly. "That's why I didn't show up, so they'd dismiss it."

"I'm sorry, Stacy, but I don't believe you."

"Look, Jonathan, what I did to you that night was wrong," she said. "I had no idea you would be arrested. I only wanted you to leave me alone."

"Then why'd you tell me to come there that night? You set me up!"

"I told you, I'm sorry."

"Why did you go to the magistrate and fill out an arrest warrant for stalking if you only wanted me to leave you alone?"

"I didn't know you'd be arrested!"

I stared at her. "How could you not know? Did you even look at the form you wrote all that nonsense on about me stalking and threatening you?"

"I remember writing down what happened on the back of a yellow piece of paper. That's all."

"Did you see the front of the form?"

"Of course I did; I had to put my name on it!"

"So you're telling me you filled out the paper but *never noticed* the big black letters on the top of the page that said 'Warrant for Arrest?'" I asked incredulously.

"Well, uh, no, I didn't see that part. I just wanted you to leave me alone."

"Stacy, I find that very hard to believe. I'm sorry, but you got what you wanted. It cost me over $5,000 and it cost you a car, but it's water under the bridge. I'm going now. I'll see you later."

I walked out the doors and was heading for my car when I noticed that Shawn was looking in my car windows.

"I see you saw Mom in there," he said as I approached.

"Yeah, I saw her."

Going back to the car, I heard Stacy say something to her son. She'd followed me out to the parking lot. I never thought to ask what she'd done with her shopping cart.

She sidled up to me and said, "So this is the new car, huh?"

"Why act like you've never seen it before? You know damn well you have. Your Mother called me at work the morning after I'd gotten it. Then a week or so later, I get a Warrant in Debt for the money she paid on bills so I'd come back to you."

"I'm sorry, I can't help what she does!"

"Yeah, well, it seems awful coincidental I'm finally able to purchase a new vehicle and *then* I get a warrant from your Mom a few days later."

"I can't help what she does," Stacy repeated.

"No, maybe not, but you sure lived and learned, huh?"

"What's that supposed to mean?" she asked, sounding hurt.

"Just forget it! You know damn well what I mean."

"Can't—can't we just talk for a while?" she whined.

"What's there to talk about? Don't you think you've done enough damage?"

I guess she didn't, because she then proceeded to fill me in on her life's progress since my arrest. She'd applied for government assistance and was placed in an apartment; she also received food stamps and Medicare through the state. She acted very proud of her accomplishments. Her Mom had evidently taken my advice and purchased Stacy a car, which I'm positive was the reasoning behind the Warrant in Debt. It was her intention that I pay for it. It only gave proof to the adage, "The apple doesn't fall far from the tree." Stacy and her Mom were always hatching some type of devious plot, one way or another.

Stacy asked me to consider coming to her apartment the next night to visit, and provided her telephone number.

I had extraordinarily mixed feelings as I drove away from the parking lot. What should I do now? Where was the therapist when I really needed him? The only thing I knew for sure as I drove home was that my ice cream was melting.

When I mentioned my chance encounter with Stacy to my parents, they were anything but happy; in fact, my Dad was so irate he threatened to call the courts and say I was in violation of my restraining order if I even *thought* about going the next night. It was a bad time for both my parents; I don't know what came over me to even entertain the idea, but I felt myself compelled to see Stacy. My Mom was crying; my Dad looking at me with disgust in his eyes. I'm not really sure how, or even when, she sunk her claws into me that night, but she did. In retrospect, I'd have to say it was a case of temporary insanity or pure stupidity, and my Dad probably should have called and reported me. The jail sentence with Bubba couldn't have been as bad as what I'd go through over the next five years.

To make a long story short, I did go to her apartment the next night, and stayed over. We had long discussions about things that had happened, and things I would not allow to happen again. Stacy was in complete agreement to all of my suggestions.

The first order of business we had to attend to was the restraining order. I went to the court and made an appointment with the Honorable Judge Howard. We drove to court together but went inside as plaintiff and defendant.

"Next case: Jonathan David and Stacy David," the Bailiff intoned.

I spoke first. "Your honor, I would like to petition the court to have the restraining order against me lifted. My wife and I would like to save our marriage, and respectfully ask the court to consider my request."

"Mrs. David," Judge Howard said, looking at her sternly, "is this also your wish, to have the restraining order removed?"

"Yes sir, it is. As my husband said, we would like to make an attempt to save our marriage."

"Very well, the order is hereby rescinded. Good luck to the both of you."

I'd always believed people could change, but I failed to consider the fact that Stacy wasn't ordinary people. For a long time, I just couldn't get this fact to stay in my head. I always wanted to give people the benefit of the doubt, and always walked away with mud on my face; you'd think I'd learn.

I was sitting in Stacy's apartment a couple days later when the phone rang. I was surprised to be receiving a phone call there; I thought it was my Mom, and was shocked to find that it was my lawyer's secretary. When she connected me to Ms. Ingram, the lawyer launched right into me: "Have you lost your mind, Jonathan? After everything that woman has put you through, all the trouble she's caused you and your family, you're back over there with her! I'm very upset with you, and so are your parents, and I don't blame them—they have every right to be!"

"I know," I said weakly.

"What about the restraining order?"

"We went to court and had it removed."

"Well, my friend, I hope you come to your senses before she really messes you up! You were lucky last time; the next time might not be in your favor. You keep that in mind!" Then she hung up on me.

I never brought it up, but I knew who'd put her up to calling me: my parents. I couldn't blame them; I'd really let everyone down. All the people who'd stood by me during my stalking ordeal, my family and friends—I'd let them all down. Worst of all, I let myself down, and couldn't explain why.

*   *   *

The next issue at hand was the Warrant in Debt that Stacy's Mom had taken out on me. I met with Stacy's parents at their attorney's office to discuss the details. I argued repeatedly that all the money was used to benefit Stacy and her kids; nothing went into my pockets, the money was offered to me as an incentive to go back with Stacy, and there was no signed agreement saying I'd pay the money back. When the meeting was over, the best deal I was able to make was pay one-half in monthly installments. Stacy would be responsible for the other. I'm sure if I'd had an attorney with me that day I'd have gotten a better deal; but I didn't have the nerve to ask Ms. Ingram to go with me to the meeting, not after what I'd just done.

I moved in with Stacy soon afterwards and everything was just like when we were first married; we actually celebrated our sixth wedding anniversary that year. However, the feelings of marital bliss would be short-lived.

We'd gone out to a nightclub on a Friday night, and then went to get something to eat afterwards. We were looking to have some fun in the bedroom when we arrived home until we found Shawn, now fifteen, in bed with a girl, also fifteen. Well, I wasn't going to allow this sort of activity to be conducted in an apartment I was living in. I certainly didn't want to be standing in front of Judge Howard again for allowing statutory rape to be committed in my presence. I cut the bedroom lights on, and stood there until both Shawn and the girl were out of the bed. I tried to get the girl to call and have her parents pick her up, but she'd lied and told her parents she was staying over at a girlfriend's. Most of the events after this point are foggy to me; I lost my composure, which is something I seldom ever do, but I went into another dimension that morning—I was completely out of my head. I don't know if it was her parents or Stacy who'd taken the girl home, but she was gone when I regained my composure. The sun was coming up; Stacy, her son and I were still arguing over what he'd done. I was completely appalled to see that Stacy was defending him; go figure, she saw nothing wrong with his actions. She'd trained him well!

Stacy had heard enough of the argument and my temper hadn't let up, so she called the police. When they arrived, I explained the situation and I was fully expecting them to commend me on my actions; I was protecting a minor, not contributing to her delinquency. Wrong again! I was the bad guy, because society says that's just the way it is. I should have known not to get between a mother and her child.

I explained to the police that Stacy and I had been up all night and I would like to go to bed and sleep it off. They wholeheartedly agreed, but I wasn't going to be sleeping there, they said. The officer informed me I *WAS* leaving the apartment to sleep, and after eight hours I could return. I was confused; why was I being punished? I was in the right! I took a stand and said adamantly that I *WAS NOT* leaving the apartment; I hadn't done anything wrong! I explained again that I would go to bed and sleep it off. The nice policemen gave me one last opportunity to walk out of there on my own, but my stubbornness was talking for me, and I heard myself say *I WAS NOT* leaving just one last time. So the officers helped me: with handcuffs and a couple of good shoves, I was out of there. They were so nice; they even gave me a free ride to the hospital in the back seat of the cruiser, and I didn't even have to ask! They must have thought I was an ungrateful person, though. I didn't appreciate their hospitality at all; I raised hell all the way.

Sometime during my brief visit to the Emergency Room, I was given something to calm me down. I must have gone to sleep, because I woke up in a "rubber" room again; but it wasn't the same one I'd been in the last time. I didn't really know where I was, but I quickly surmised I didn't want to be there, and I wasn't very happy. I should have listened to the nice policeman and left the apartment that morning.

I must have been very hungry for knowledge that day, because I soon learned a second lesson: don't bang on the little glass window in the rubber room door for hours on end. It only pisses people off, especially the ones who can make important decisions as to your welfare. Once I'd gotten the attention of everyone on the floor, including the other patients, I was finally let out of the room with the pretense that I could use the telephone; but they tricked me. I was taken to another room, one that resembled Dr. Frankenstein's basement, the room where he created and kept his monster. It came fully equipped with a big table and leather straps to tie down both my hands and feet.

12

I'm Not the One Wearing Handcuffs!

I don't have the slightest clue as to how long I lay in Dr. Frankenstein's laboratory, strapped to the bed; the good doctor had given me some pretty powerful drugs, I was sure. I vaguely remember someone coming in there and feeding me some kind of a rice dish. Once I was awake and my feeding orderly was gone, I started wondering what I'd do if I had to go to the bathroom. How I was supposed to accomplish that feat I had absolutely no idea; screaming and yelling had gotten me put in here in the first place. Luckily, someone came in before I had a call of nature, probably because the drugs I'd been injected with slowed down my bodily functions. I was unshackled and allowed to put on my pants before they took me down a hall and put me in a normal room. They allowed me to use the bathroom facilities; of course I was observed as I did so, then was told to get into the bed and was given another shot.

I awoke the next morning with very little memory of anything that had happened since being placed in the bondage bed. It was very lonely there; besides me, there was only one other person in my section, an older woman. I found out from one of my friendly attendants that I did have a roommate, but he was locked up in another "rubber" room on suicide watch; he'd decided to drink a bottle of shampoo.

I went to the end of the hall and found that the door was locked from the other side. It didn't take a genius to realize I was in the isolation ward. There was a telephone on the wall, but when

I checked, there wasn't a dial tone. At the end of the hall, by the locked doors on the right hand side, was the office where all the facility's personnel stayed. I could see another hall on the other side of the office through the glass. People were coming and going into a community room eating popsicles and what appeared to be frozen juice cups. There were no popsicles in my community room; it didn't even have a refrigerator. We did have the luxury of a television, but it was high on the wall, and we had to wait for someone to come into the isolation ward to change the channel. We did have a table and chairs where we could eat our meals, and a sofa.

The older woman never spoke the whole time I was there.

Most of the information I learned came from the people on the other side. On every even hour, starting at eight in the morning and ending at ten at night, I was let out and allowed to go into a small room on the other hallway with the others to smoke a cigarette. There were eight to ten people crammed into a room that would comfortably accommodate four. Before I went in I'd go to the office window and be handed one cigarette before they unlocked the door and let me out.

There was a small electrical apparatus on the wall, and you'd put your cigarette inside the small hole and push a button until the cigarette lit; it was very similar to a car cigarette lighter. Most of the people coming in would use someone else's lit smoke to light theirs, rather than use the wall; it didn't work most of the time anyway, since all it took was a paperclip to short it out. My first visit that morning was interesting.

"Are you the one who kept knocking on the window of that room over there?" one guy asked.

"Yes, that was me," I admitted.

"You sure gave them a workout; you had 'em in and out quite often."

"Yeah, I guess I pissed 'em off. They put me in the other room and restrained me."

"Yeah, we know. We watched when they put you in there."

"So, how do I get from that side to this side? You guys seem to be free to roam; I can't do anything but pace the halls. I have a roommate, someone said, but I haven't seen him."

"He's in that other room over there next to where you were restrained. He tried to drink shampoo."

"Yeah, that's what I heard."

One of the orderlies came, said time was up, and back to isolation I went. Out of curiosity I checked the phone again, and this time there was a dial tone. They evidently cut the phone off at night and cut it back on in the morning. I dialed Stacy's apartment but got the answering machine, so I left a message thanking her for arranging for me to stay in this five-star resort; in fact, I left quite a few nice messages. I told her how I couldn't believe she'd stooped to such a low level. None of the messages were threatening by any means, as I later found out I was accused of.

There was a chart on the wall that listed the rights of the patient. When I questioned some of these rights, the orderly told me I was being held as a ward of the state on a temporary detaining order for seventy-two hours and I had no rights, so the chart didn't apply to me. I'd been there twenty-four hours or more, and asked if I could go to the other side. I was told absolutely not; there were no available beds on that side. I knew that was complete bullshit. To prove my point, I asked if I could wander around over there and sleep on the side I was on, but that was also refused. I asked if I could have a popsicle, and again no luck. I decided it would not be in my best interests to ask why I was allowed to smoke with them; I might lose that one privilege if I kept trying to push their buttons. I'll bet if Stacy were there, she'd have manipulated her way over to the other side in no time.

Soon, the highlight of each day was watching the clock for the even hours, so I could go smoke.

I learned a lot in my communications with the people on the other side during the smoke breaks. I'll admit, I wasn't very happy to be there under the circumstances. But after talking with some of the people in the smoking lounge, I discovered that I was fortunate enough to have good insurance benefits—something I suppose

I'd taken for granted, and never given much thought to. Most of the people on the other side, I soon learned, had self-admitted themselves to the psychiatric unit. I'd never been in this type of environment before, and naturally thought they were having issues with relationships or coping with societal problems; maybe their boyfriends, girlfriends, wives, etc. had left them or they were unable to procure work. Again, I was naïve.

After hearing their stories in the few short minutes we were able to communicate with each other, I began to feel sorry for most of them. They had no insurance at all, and all were suffering from different forms of depression or anxiety disorders. The cost of their medications far exceeded their paychecks, and they were unable to buy their medications on a regular basis. Most said the same things: they had to make a month's supply of medicine last two months or longer. During these times, if things became too difficult, they would self-admit themselves for five to seven days, get their bodies back on track with medication, then go back out and maintain for another six to eight weeks until they'd have to repeat the procedure. You'd think the state would have some type of program in place to help people in this condition with their monthly medications; the cost of their medicines couldn't be as expensive as the cost of a stay in the unit, which the state would ultimately absorb.

I hadn't had much luck contacting Stacy on the telephone; it seems she didn't want to talk to me. After leaving numerous messages over the past few days, she'd called the unit and had one of the orderlies come and advise me that she wanted me to please stop trying to contact her. I'd soon find out that wasn't all she'd told the unit workers!

I was able to contact my parents, and they came one night during visitation hours; I was even allowed to go to the grown-up community room on the other side for visitation. I'd asked them to bring me a couple packs of cigarettes so I could replace the ones I'd been smoking. I hadn't given it any thought, but my Dad asked me to give him the keys to my car so he could go to Stacy's apartment and pick it up. She had the spare set, and undoubtedly was tooling around town while she'd imprisoned me in a mental facility. I should have thought of it sooner but hadn't; cars seemed to be Stacy's weakness.

That night after their visit, the car was picked up from her apartment and taken back to their home. On the third day, hopefully my last, an orderly came to me early and advised me they'd be coming to get me in a few minutes for a special hearing being conducted in my honor. This was one of the benefits of being in isolation; the people on the other side didn't get special hearings in their honor. They had to settle for popsicles. The orderly also advised me I had a phone call; I was told to stand by the phone in the hallway, and they'd transfer the call.

It was Stacy, of course; the car had been taken away.

"Why did your parents come and pick up your car?" she asked bluntly, with an obvious tone of anger in her voice.

"Because it's my car, Stacy. Now, why aren't you taking my calls? I've left messages and you never respond, but you call up here and you have them tell me to stop calling you!"

"Because I'm mad at you for the way you acted, that's why. You don't seem to realize that you could have put my son in juvenile detention!"

"Oh, I'm so sorry for having morals, Stacy! May the good Lord strike me dead if your precious, innocent son gets in trouble for statutory rape; but you didn't think twice about having your husband, your meal ticket, put away, now did you?"

"I can see you still have an attitude!"

"Stacy, I didn't call the police. You did. I was only doing what I knew was right. Had you not called the police, this never would have happened—and I believe you're missing the point completely. Shawn put himself in the situation, and you defended him. What would you have done if Suzy was fifteen and caught in bed with another teenager? Wouldn't you have been concerned about your daughter's welfare and reputation? You're damn right you would have, and I bet if that girl's parents knew what went on that night, they'd applaud me for stopping it! But then again, they may not have morals and a sense of decency like I do. But I'm sure they do;

she certainly didn't want to call her parents that morning. She knew what she was doing was wrong."

"Well, I need the car, so call your Dad and have him bring it back!"

"No. You put me here, so suffer the consequences. I have a hearing today, and I should get released. We'll discuss it then."

"Are you going to get the car back here today or not?"

"That all depends on what happens to me today at my hearing. When the car comes back to your apartment, I'll be driving it, not before. You have a car."

"Suzy has it, and said she'll bring it back when she feels like it."

"Stacy, who's the parent and who's the child?"

"Damn you, you bastard!"

The monotonous hum of the dial tone was the next sound I heard; she'd hung up on me, as usual. I'd be willing to bet she threw the phone at the wall, too.

I went back to my suite and waited until they came to escort me to my hearing, where I was surprised to see my Mom; she'd been invited as character witness.

When the young attorney started reading off the accounts of the occurrences from the time the police were called to the apartment until the present, I was completely taken aback. Stacy had called the unit and told them I'd called her apartment and left a message saying I was going to kill her and her kids. When given a chance to speak on my own behalf, I denied making any such threatening calls, and asked if they'd heard this so-called threatening message—which, of course, they hadn't. They were taking the she-devil's word over mine again. My Mom said it was entirely against my nature to do any such thing; I wasn't a violent person. The judge conducting the hearing, however, wasn't convinced by my statement; and after weighing out the severity of Stacy's accusations, he didn't feel comfortable releasing me. I was sentenced to thirty more days at another hospital.

Stacy had dreamed up an excellent scheme to keep me away. I later found out that her son had sought revenge against me for making his girlfriend leave that morning, and told his Mom I'd been having an affair with a woman I'd met at a nearby McDonald's drive-thru window. Of course, with him being such a sweet and loving child, she believed him—ergo the make-believe threats. Stacy's plan had been beautifully orchestrated, and worked perfectly until my Dad had taken the car away; then she realized her plan had backfired. I might be away another thirty days, and she needed transportation. Suzy had commandeered her car, and Stacy wouldn't stand her ground and take it back. It was always about cars!

It was time for the transformation from Mrs. Hyde to Dr. Jekyll again.

Since it had been determined that I would be leaving their fine establishment and I hadn't caused any trouble since I'd been placed into my room a couple days ago, the staff of the facility allowed to me to stay outside the solitary wing and congregate with the others. They'd also let my roommate out of his isolation room, and I saw him for the first time. I was still upset that I hadn't been granted my freedom and released, but at least I wouldn't be placed in solitary confinement where I was going. The hospital in which I was currently staying didn't have a counseling program set up for long-term, extended stays, so I was being transferred to another area hospital that did offer those services. I was told a Sheriff's deputy from my hometown would be transporting me to the other facility, and he'd be arriving in a couple of hours.

I wasn't allowed to walk out of the psychiatric unit; I had to sit in a wheelchair, and was once again shackled and cuffed for the ride in the deputy's car. I'd always wondered why they even bother to place a sheet over your chest and feet when transporting inmates through the hospital's corridors. I always thought the police officer was pushing someone who been grotesquely burned on his hands and feet, and the sheet was to hide the hideous sight from other staff, patients and visitors. Now I know why the sheet is there, if the person is being pushed by an officer of the law.

Once inside the deputy's car on the way to the other hospital, I tried to engage him in conversation, but he just wasn't interested in talking to someone of my class. "I know the Sheriff personally," I mentioned.

"I do too," he said, in a smart-ass tone.

"He's good friends with my family."

"Well, good for you!"

It was no use; he was undoubtedly a better class of person than I. He'd already judged me as a guilty lowlife without knowing the details; innocent until proven guilty, my ass! To add further insult to injury, he reached into his pocket and pulled out a cigarette and lit it.

"Could I have one, please?" I asked.

"No!" he said emphatically.

"I don't think it's nice that you can smoke but I can't."

"I'm not the one wearing handcuffs."

Touché; I was guilty as hell in his eyes. It was no use even trying to carry on a casual conversation, so I decided I'd be quiet for the rest of the ride; isn't that what criminals do?

Upon arriving at the other hospital, we repeated the sheet-and-wheelchair routine. I was taken to the third floor on an elevator that could only be operated by pushing a button which sounded a bell on the third floor. The third floor staff would then go to the elevator, insert a key into the wall switch, and call the elevator up. Once on the floor, my restraints were removed and I was escorted to an office to answer a series of questions. It was extremely embarrassing to be recognized by the woman asking the questions, as she was a neighbor of my parents.

This facility was a lot nicer than the other; I was allowed to roam as I pleased on the floor, and snacks and juices were always available. There was a smoking booth available with no time restrictions. To my amazement, they also had frozen juices in the freezer; it must be a mental institution tradition.

I'd been there about for about two hours when another guest informed me that I had a call on the payphone. It was Stacy.

"What are you doing there?" she demanded. "I thought you were being released! I called the other hospital, and they told me you'd been transferred."

"Yeah, I thought I'd be released too, until I found out I had homicidal tendencies towards you and the kids. Someone must have seen my face on 'America's Most Wanted' and called in a tip. The judge sent me here for thirty days."

"I didn't do that!"

"You didn't do what, Stacy?"

"I didn't say you were going to *kill* anyone!"

"The attorney at my hearing begs to differ. He distinctly said you did."

"B-but, I just said I was scared you'd be so mad when you got out that you might want to kill me and the kids, Jonathan. I was only kidding!"

"Statements like that are *not* taken in a joking manner, dammit!"

"I'm sorry!" she wailed.

I sighed. "It's too late for that, Stacy. I don't believe you anyhow."

"Look, Jonny, Shawn said you were having an affair with a woman at the McDonalds drive-through. I got mad and called and said what I did. I'm sorry!"

"And you believed him?" I growled, outraged.

"At the time I did, but then Suzy told me he made the whole story up to get back at you for making his girlfriend leave. I'm so sorry, honey; can you forgive me?"

"Not right now, no!"

"Can you arrange for me to pick your car up at your parents, or have them bring it to the hospital and I'll get Suzy to bring me there and then drive your car home?"

"*No.* I don't even want to talk to you right now. When I do, I'll call you. Goodbye."

I met a few people who were in the same position as I—in relationships that had gone badly. We played cards, talked, laughed, and went to group classes. It was actually an enlightening experience for me. I thought I had it bad, until I heard stories from the others. Many seemed to be hurting worse than I. I'd become too classically conditioned to the abuse; I saw it as a normal way of life and had grown to accept it, whereas the others were experiencing many of these things for the first time. Later, I wished I'd never had that realization. It caused me to soften up on Stacy, and I found myself trying to justify her actions again. Maybe it was true that she'd only made that threatening call because her son had lied. But why had she called the police that morning in the first place? Was she only trying to protect her son? It was the first time she'd ever seen my temper; maybe I'd scared her. Before the day was over; I found myself calling my parents and asking them to please bring the car to the hospital when they visited, so Stacy could pick it up when she came to visit. That was a very bad mistake.

I believe that if my Dad had had his will handy at that time, I'd have been eradicated from it. I did ask, later, if the thought had ever entered his mind, and wasn't surprised when he said that it had. However, he said he wouldn't have excluded me entirely—he'd simply have taken the necessary steps to put my sister in charge of my inheritance as long as I was married to Stacy. I can't say I blamed him; I had thoroughly disgusted him again. I just wouldn't learn. I also believe he wouldn't have come to see me, if it weren't for my Mom urging him to do so. I don't really know for sure. I was scared to ask, and never did. They did come to visit, and Stacy happened to call while they were there; it was definitely an awkward moment. She made a point to have me say "I love you" for them to hear. They said they'd bring the car on the next visitation, that Thursday night.

The Black Widow had me thinking about her lair again. As soon as I could be released from the hospital I knew I'd go crawling back. I called her after my parents left. "My parents will have the car here Thursday night," I told her.

"Great! I'll try to come see you. If I can't make it, can you send the keys downstairs and I pick them up?"

"No, you have to come and get them. I'm locked in here, and there are no exceptions. Visitation isn't until Thursday night, so you can't get the keys until then."

"But I need the car tomorrow! Can I go to your parents' and pick it up?"

"Now, what do *you* think, Stacy? After what you've done to me, do you really want to go to their house and set foot on their property, much less ring the doorbell and ask for the keys?"

"No." She was silent for a long moment. "Can't they leave the keys in the car?"

"Why don't you call and ask them?"

"I'm not calling over there!"

"Then I'm sorry. Thursday night is the earliest you can get it."

"Dammit!" she spat and hung up.

Later that afternoon, I was taken to see the psychiatrist assigned to the psych floor that particular day. I sure wish the police had taken me there first. Once she introduced herself to me and we went through the ritual of suicidal questions, I told her of my ordeal.

"So . . . your wife is Stacy David, correct?" she asked suspiciously.

"Yes. I thought your name sounded familiar. Stacy's called you numerous times on weekends to get Xanax, hasn't she?"

"I'm not allowed to discuss that, Mr. David."

"I know, sorry for asking. Do you see anything wrong with my actions that morning, making the girl call her parents and all?"

"No, I don't. You did the right thing."

"Then why am I here?"

"Mr. David, if you'd have been brought here instead and told me the story you just told me, I'd have let you sleep it off and sent you home the next day. However, the judge ordered you to serve thirty days, and now the best I can do is release you in three or four days. I'm sorry, but it's all I can do under the circumstances."

"It's okay, Doctor, I'm not having a bad time here. In fact, this is kind of like a vacation for me. Being around others with similar problems makes me realize I'm not alone, and my problems seem minor in comparison to some of the stories I've been told here."

She nodded. "If everything goes well I'll let you go home on Friday, unless of course you feel you'd like to stay longer?"

"No, Friday will be fine."

I called Stacy on that day, Wednesday, to let her know I expected to be released by the doctor on Friday, but I could stay longer if I wanted. I also asked if she'd be coming Thursday night for visitation.

"Yes, I'll be there," she said. "I just have to find a ride."

"Why don't you drive your own car?"

"Suzy has plans and she uses it a lot."

"Why don't you stand up to her? You're the parent, Stacy."

"Jonathan, please don't start, okay? This hasn't been a good week for me!"

"Oh, I'm so sorry, Stacy; my week has been just perfect. I can be *so* inconsiderate at times."

"You don't ever stop, do you? I said I was *sorry.*"

I brushed aside her apology. "You'll have to be here Friday at noon to pick me up."

"Okay, Jonny. Honey, is there any way possible you could get your parents to bring the car today and leave it in the parking lot? They could leave the keys at the information desk."

"You call and ask them; I won't."

"No, that's quite all right."

"I thought so. I told the staff you'd be here to pick me up on Friday. If you're not coming, let me know now, so I can make other arrangements."

"Oh, I'll be there. I'll let you know when I pick the car up tomorrow night."

"Stacy, if you're not coming to visit me, you won't be picking up the car. I'll drive it home when I leave on Friday."

"But what if I can't make it in time for visitation?"

"Then don't bother coming at all."

My failure to retreat back to the controllable person I had been was reaping its benefits now. Stacy saw that I might be evolving into a force to be reckoned with; I'd had enough of her games.

During my Thursday afternoon talk with the psychiatrist, I explained the signs of abuse I'd been through so far. "I thought I had a good handle on her control and manipulation games, doctor, but obviously I was mistaken, since I wound up in here."

"But you're recognizing her methods now, and that's a good thing. Once she realizes you're trying to reestablish control of the situation, she'll retaliate; it's a defensive measure on her part. She's not used to one of her victims striking back, and you seem to be a real threat to her now. My advice is to keep on your toes. She'll be watching your every move, just as you're watching hers. It's getting down to a trust issue for you, and she's going to be constantly on guard; you're tearing down her 'web,' as you call it."

"She's trying to destroy my self-esteem by making me believe I'm a worthless person that no one else would consider having," I said. "But I do realize she's only trying to exercise another sign of abuse, and I'm not a bad person at all."

"That's a sign of her own insecurities."

"I know. My therapist and I came to the same conclusion. If anything, she's the evil one trying to project her feelings of worthlessness onto me. She'd tried desperately to alienate me from my family, but blood is thicker than water, and they're sticking by me. Granted, they're not always happy, but they've remained true to me."

"That's great!"

"As far as her threats and accusations go, I've learned they only work if I react to them. To her, my trying to defend myself is only misinterpreted as a defense mechanism to hide my guilt. If I simply look at her with an 'I'm not even going to respond to your ridiculous statement' expression it drives her crazy; she doesn't know what I'm thinking."

"Well, Jonathan, it seems the therapy sessions have done you well," the psychiatrist declared. "You have a very good insight into your situation. So—do you think you have a grip on the issues now?"

I shrugged. "I'm not saying I can't still be coerced, but I believe I can handle myself better. I'm still worried about physical abuse towards me; it hasn't happened yet, and hopefully it won't, but I can't help but read the handwriting on the wall, Doctor. I believe it's just around the corner."

"Let's hope for your sake it doesn't happen. Now, I'm releasing you tomorrow at noon. Have you made arrangements for someone to pick you up?"

"Yes, I have. Stacy's coming to see me tonight, and she'll pick me up tomorrow"

She looked at me for a long moment before saying, "Good luck, my friend."

Stacy did show up that night for visitation, and brought me candy; but the nurses took it away. We weren't allowed any 'energy' food.

As promised, I was released the next day, and wonder of wonders, Stacy was there to pick me up. She took me back to her apartment, and we went back to our life together.

*   *   *

Stacy would never change for the better; I knew it was wishful thinking to ever think that could happen. Therefore, I could only focus my hopes on another possibility: that she wouldn't get any worse. The optimistic side of me wanted to keep the possibility alive, but her substance abuse worsened considerably; and when her pill supply ran low, her violent tendencies began escalating to an even higher degree. My only saving grace was that I hadn't seen very many signs of physical abuse . . . yet. But as it turned out, I would be in for the ride of my life during the next few years, and I'd soon grow to despise the woman I'd once been crazy about. The woman I'd married had ceased to exist; she'd been completely overtaken by a demon.

I've always heard mistakes can be beneficial, that they build character. I've also heard if something doesn't kill you, it only makes you stronger. It's funny how life's lessons can finally make you see things from a different perspective, especially when your life is in the hands of a higher power and barely hanging by a thread.

Life was moving on as usual when I arrived back at Stacy's apartment; however, I still harbored angry feelings towards both Stacy and Shawn. I hadn't been back more than fifteen minutes when the boy started toying with me and trying to get under my skin. "Did you have a nice vacation?" he asked.

"Are you trying to be *funny?*" I snarled.

"Not really. What's the matter? Can't you take a joke?"

"Shawn, let me make this perfectly clear: your Mother told me what you accused me of, and I don't think it's the least bit funny!"

"It was only a joke, man, lighten up!"

"I'll remember your comment when the ball is in *my* court, and you're on the other side of the locked doors!"

"What's that supposed to mean?"

"You'll find out. You think it's hilarious that I had to spend six days in a mental institution, don't you? And all of it was because your mother called and made some very harmful accusations about me based on your lies!"

"I said it was a joke, man, let it go!"

"I'll let it go for now, *man*. But one day the shoe's going to be on the other foot, and I'll remind you of this moment. I spent six days locked on a mental floor, but six days wasn't that bad when I consider that it could have been *years*. I'll never put myself in that situation again. But you're of the age now where your Mama won't always be able to bail you out of trouble, and you may soon find yourself a ward of the state. You could end up serving a whole lot more than six days. So you go ahead and continue living your life and making up lies, thinking you're above the law—but when you cross that fine line between legal and illegal, it'll be out of your Mom's hands. And when that moment comes, we'll see how much faith a judge puts in your claim that it's 'only a joke.' The judge will always take the word of the man wearing a badge over yours."

"I'm not scared of that badge. It don't mean shit to me, man!"

"I'll remind you that you said that, too, kiddo."

"Jonathan, let it go!" Stacy piped up, "he said he was sorry!"

"No, he didn't. He said it was only a joke."

"Shawn, tell him you're sorry!" Stacy demanded.

"No," I interjected, "I don't want his damn apology. You're just as much to blame as he is, Stacy. *You're* the one who called the hospital and said I was going to kill the whole family, a story you *made up* based on his lies! His lies, and your believing him, caused me to spend an additional four days in a hospital."

"Oh, Jonny, I'm sorry I called and said those things!" Stacy cried. "I was just mad."

"Well, that makes it okay, doesn't it?" I didn't let her respond. "Right now I'm mad at both of you, so just drop it before the police get called again. The next time I'm told by 'the badge' to leave this apartment, I won't be coming back; not because I'll be in jail, but because it'll be my personal choice! The both of you pushed me just a little too far this time."

It was a Friday night, and the more I saw that silly-ass smirk on Shawn's face; the angrier I got. Stacy suggested we go out to the nightclub. "C'mon, it'll give you a chance to drink a few beers, loosen up, and relax a little; maybe blow off a little steam. There's a good band there this week."

"Yeah, maybe so, but no overnight guests. If I come home and find him in the bed with another girl this time, I'll be the one calling the police *and* someone's parents!"

"We've already had a talk about that, Jonny. He knows now that what he did was wrong and that he put both you and me in a bad situation."

"Would you really do that? Call the police?" Shawn demanded.

"Try me and see."

"Okay, that's enough!" Stacy said. "Shawn, you leave him alone—and Jonny, go get your shower."

We went out that evening and I tried to have a good time, but it just wasn't working. Stacy looked pretty good and was trying to be romantic towards me, but I couldn't help but think about the fact that last Friday night I'd been in the same place, having a good time—but 12 hours later I was locked up inside a mental facility. Those thoughts alone dampened my spirits; my heart just wasn't in it that night, and I knew I was still carrying feelings of resentment towards Stacy.

"What's wrong, baby?" she asked during a slow dance.

"Oh, I'm just not feeling very festive tonight. I guess the last week took its toll on me, and I have a lot of thinking to do. I have to come to terms with what happened."

"Okay, let's go sit down and talk about it."

"This isn't the place, Stacy. Maybe we should just leave and go home."

"No, get it off your chest; just say what's on your mind. I don't want to carry this problem home."

"Fine. If you get mad, don't say I didn't warn you."

We walked off the dance floor and returned to our table. It was neither the time nor place to have this discussion, but she insisted, so I went with it.

"Stacy, I just can't help but feel uncomfortable holding you on the dance floor, when only a week ago you called the hospital and told them I was going to kill your whole family. I don't believe you understand the psychological impact this last week has had on me."

She said sympathetically, "Yes, I know you're taking it hard, and I'm truly sorry."

I shook my head sadly. "Stacy, I don't think you completely understand. I've lost a lot of respect for you; and to be perfectly frank, I just don't know if I can ever trust you again. What happens the next time I make you mad? What then, Stacy? I was arrested based on fabricated facts, placed in a mental institution for standing up for what I know was the moral thing to do, and then to have that stay extended again based on lies! What is it going to be next time, a jail cell?"

"Jonny, I understand your anger. What I did was wrong, okay? I know that. I should have never listened to Shawn. I know he doesn't always tell the truth."

"You *don't* understand, Stacy; you're missing the point here completely. You know he *always* lies yet you never even questioned what he said; you just took him at his word and acted on it. Why did you call and say I threatened to kill all of you? That's a *very* serious charge! That judge could have easily sent me to jail that day. You should have known better! You're an adult, but your actions were those of a child who ran home to tell Daddy somebody called you a bad name. You don't make up lies to judges, Stacy! If I could have proven the accusations were false, don't you realize you could have been arrested for making false accusations, very serious false accusations? Did that ever enter your mind?"

"I'm sorry, Jonny! You're right! I should have known better. I realize that now; doesn't that count?"

"In my opinion, you didn't realize you'd screwed up until my Dad came and took the car away. That's when you realized you'd made a mistake. *Then* your mistake bought me four more days! It should have been thirty. You weren't counting on that happening, were you?"

"Okay, okay, I see your point!"

"Stacy, hindsight is 20/20, but what about the future? How do I know you're not going to do something like this again? You can sit here and tell me you won't until pigs fly, but I don't know if I can ever believe you again. You took away a week of my life for complete bullshit, and I'm sorry to say I don't see you showing any signs of remorse!"

"What is it you want me to do, Jonny? Tell me! How can I make this up to you?"

"You can't. You can't turn back time, Stacy. That time is lost, and will never be replaced. First it was stalking because you were mad, then this. What's next?"

"I'm sorry! Really, I'm truly sorry! Can we just put it behind us and move on?"

At that point I knew I just wanted to go home. I didn't want to be there that night. I'm not sure if I even wanted to be there with her. I watched as she went into her pocketbook and took out the pill bottle. *Here we go!* I thought. *When life comes at you fast, pop a couple Xanax; it makes things better.* I think she took 2 mgs.

Another slow song was playing, and she asked if we could dance again. Reluctantly, I agreed. I felt somewhat better after getting everything off my chest, and she hadn't blown up at me; deep down, I guess she knew she had it coming. The night improved slightly, but I still just wanted to go home, which we finally did. I told her all I wanted to do was get good night's sleep, that maybe I'd feel better tomorrow. I hadn't slept well in the hospitals, except for the one night when Dr. Frankenstein gave me the shot. Sex was the farthest thing on my mind at that time. I had to make resolutions; I had to come to terms with everything, with myself.

Stacy must have known she'd pushed me to my limits. When I woke the next morning, she'd already gotten up and the bedroom door was closed. I could hear her in the other room telling the kids to be quiet, I was trying to sleep. When I did get up and come out of the bedroom, Stacy immediately got up and fixed me a cup of coffee. The smirk on Shawn's face was gone and Suzy, her daughter, was sitting on the couch.

"Are you glad to be home?" Suzy asked.

"I guess so. I never should have had to leave."

"Well, I just want to let you know, I told Mom that crap about the McDonalds drive-through wasn't true."

"Really? Did you tell her before or *after* she told the hospital I was going to kill all of you?"

"I didn't know about that until after she'd made the call."

"How'd you sleep, honey?" Stacy asked brightly.

"Good. It felt good to be back in my own bed."

"It felt good having you there beside me," she said silkily. "Now, what would you like to do today?"

"Nothing. I don't want to do anything but sit at home and relax. I've had a very trying week."

"Do you want to go out tonight?" she asked. "Maybe we'll have a better time than last night."

"I don't know. I'll think about it and let you know."

"Okay, sweetie!"

I knew then that she was terrified that I was considering packing my stuff and leaving. The thought had actually entered my mind quite a few times the previous night at the club. My gut feeling told me that my going to sleep last night and having no thoughts of sex had clued her in. She knew I could walk away and there would be no recourse; she was still living in government housing and she'd survived before I came back. There was nothing holding me there.

However, good ol' Stacy was always a step ahead of the game. She'd already devised a plan, and would be acting on it very soon!

13

My Stained Glass
Window is Gone!

Stacy's plan to keep me from walking away was actually legitimate. She was living in government-assisted housing, and my being there knocked the household income out of range, especially since Stacy didn't have any income at all. Rather than gamble and get caught, she suggested we look for somewhere else to live. She'd already informed the office that we had gotten back together, and would be leaving as soon as we could find a place. I was tired of renting and wanted to see an investment on my money, but I knew my options were limited—very limited. Buying a home was out of the question, since Stacy's assistance in damaging my credit score ensured I wouldn't qualify for a conventional mortgage unless I wanted to pay exorbitant interest rates. We decided to check into purchasing a mobile home. They weren't necessarily considered investment property, but the qualifying regulations weren't as stringent as traditional home mortgages. I did qualify for a loan, but the down payment was higher than I'd expected, and therefore I couldn't take it on.

So we drove around several mobile home parks until we found a fairly new mobile home listed for rent by the owner. I called the number and arranged to meet the owners later that evening. They were an older couple and very nice, but I could tell they were very particular about their home; it was spotless, and still retained that new home smell. They explained they were tired of living in the park and had rented a house nearby. We signed a contract to rent, and worked out a rent-with-option-to-buy plan. We moved in just prior to Thanksgiving in 1999.

Things were relatively quiet for a while. I was working some overtime and money was tight, but sufficient to pay the bills. My co-workers had a good time joking about my moving into a trailer park; in fact, they were taking bets as to how long it would be before Stacy and I were guests on the *Jerry Springer Show*. I had no choice but to play along; I'd learned long before that if you let them know they're getting to you, it only gets worse.

Y2K was fast approaching, and was the talk of the news media. Christmas came and went without a major crisis. Stacy and I stayed at home on New Year's Eve to see if the big disasters everyone predicted would happen, but of course they didn't.

I didn't have a computer at that time, as they were still a bit pricey—I was the sole source of income, and my budget couldn't handle any more expenses. But soon after the first of the year, my employer contracted with a local computer technology group to provide computers to the employees. The payments would be deducted from our paychecks in small weekly installments over a two-year period. I could afford the seven or eight dollar weekly payment, so I took advantage of the opportunity and ordered my first computer. Looking back, I now see that as *another* major mistake.

I was very inexperienced with the Internet, and was completely naïve as to the types of sites people could get into. It was one of my co-workers who best described the Internet to me: "Imagine walking into the biggest Wal-Mart in the world, and everything you could ever think of or want is in there."

I watched Shawn as he 'surfed the web' and I admit, I was surprised at the information out there for anybody to access. But my naivety was mild compared to Stacy's; she just didn't understand things such as 'cookies,' which I would soon begin to understand. But she quickly learned about and loved EBay! I'd come home and my online mailbox would be loaded with email, all from EBay. I promptly deleted the ones that said, 'You've been outbid,' but there were still many that said 'You've won item #__!' Then there were the ones that said 'You've been sent an Invoice from___'; there were lots of those.

One day I looked at all the emails and groaned, "Stacy, what did you do? What the hell did you buy?"

"I won some auctions today; I had a lot of fun!"

"Yes, I can see that. Exactly how many did you win?"

"Four or five maybe. I'm not really sure."

I counted and found she'd won a total of sixteen, which were matched to sixteen emails from people wanting their money. When I added it all up, included the shipping charges, it was a little over $200. Stacy had gotten caught up in the bidding game, and won auctions for $7 or $8 for items that probably only cost $4 or $5. Factoring in the shipping cost, she could have bought two in a regular store for what it cost to buy and ship each item. Needless to say, I was not happy. "Where are you going to get the money to pay for all of this, Stacy?" I demanded.

"Well, you get paid tomorrow, don't you?"

"Yes, but the power and phone bills are due this week; what the hell were you thinking, buying all this stuff? You don't need it. Why'd you buy it?"

"I don't know," she said defensively. "I was winning until the last minute or two, then I'd get outbid and that made me mad, so I bid higher to make sure I won. It was fun!"

"Was it worth $220 to buy stuff you could buy at Wal-Mart for less than $30?"

She huffed, "Can't you wait to pay the light bill and phone bills next week?"

I decided I'd beat her at her own game; she wasn't quite sure how the computer worked anyway. She couldn't do any damage if she didn't have a phone to connect with.

"I'll pay the power bill and pay for all these damn auctions, but don't you do that again!" I snapped.

"I'm sorry, Jonny, I just got caught up in the moment. I'll be more careful next time!"

"Stacy, there won't be a next time unless I *agree* to let you bid on things. If we don't need it, you don't bid!"

She glared at me for a long time. "Why don't you just kiss my ass!" she finally said.

I knew it was coming; it was only a matter of time. She'd been calm since before Christmas, about two weeks ago, a classic sign her Xanax supply was getting low.

As I said earlier, I was naïve about computers; Shawn, however, was pretty knowledgeable. For example, until then, I thought Spam was the stuff you bought at the grocery store in the blue cans, and Stacy thought the same thing; for once, both of us were in agreement in our ignorance.

I came home from work the next day, and Stacy met me at the front door. The look on her face told me she was terribly upset about something. Being computer illiterate at the time, I had no idea what was coming.

"I'd like for you to explain something to me," she said.

"Okay, what?"

"Let me show you. Come on."

I followed her into the bedroom where the computer was located, and she had my mailbox open. "Who is Elizabeth and why does she want to meet you, Jonathan?" she demanded.

"I have no idea who Elizabeth is; what the hell are you talking about?"

She opened the email and I saw, 'Hi Jonathan; my name is Elizabeth and I've been dying to meet you! Click on this link and let's chat!"

Oh, shit! What the hell is this? I thought frantically. "I have no idea what this is about, Stacy. Seriously, I don't know what that is."

"You've got some explaining to do, buddy!"

What was I supposed to say to her? I knew that when Stacy referred to me as 'buddy,' it always meant trouble. I went to work the next day after a long night of the silent treatment, and a co-worker explained how my e-mail box got bombarded with junk mail or spam. "Every time you go onto a website," he explained, "you leave behind little tracks, what they call 'cookies.'"

"Yeah, I've heard the term 'cookies' before. One time a window opened on the screen and said I had to enable 'cookies' to visit certain sites," I told him.

"That's right, and from these 'cookies', people can get your email address and sometimes the name it's registered under. How many e-mail addresses do you have?"

"Just the one, the one the computer place gave me."

"Did you make a separate email address for your wife and her kids?"

"No, I didn't know I could do that."

"It's easy. You need to create email addresses for each of them, everyone will have their own password, and you keep your password private so they can't get online using your name."

"What about EBay? That seems to be a problem, too."

"Change your password. If they want to play on EBay, then let them register under their own names so they can't access your account."

"Great idea!"

I went home and told Stacy what he'd told me about 'cookies' and 'tracks' and people being able to get your name from them. She didn't want to hear it; there were more pressing matters at hand, and I had more explaining to do.

I don't know where Shawn had been going, I didn't know anything about computer history, and I had no idea how to clean out what they called a 'cache.' As I said, I was ignorant as hell with computers.

"Follow me!" Stacy said, and led me to the bedroom again, "Let me see you talk your way out of this one!"

I looked on the screen and saw a photo of a scantily clad woman in an email, and the caption said, 'Would you like to meet exciting singles in your area for fun tonight?'

"Uh oh!" I said out loud.

"Yes, 'uh oh' is right. Would you care to explain, you lying bastard?"

"Stacy, I don't know what to tell you. I haven't been anywhere like that. Who else has been on this computer?"

"Shawn and me! I'm glad he didn't see this filth."

"Do you think it's possible he's going into porn sites, and that's where the emails are coming from?"

"Oh, that's good, Jonathan. Shift the blame to a fifteen year old!"

"Shawn, come in here!" When he did, I demanded, "Have you been going into porn sites?"

"I don't know how to get to those!" he said, but I knew he was lying; his eyes gave him away.

"Okay, I'm going to fix this. My friend at work told me to set up separate email addresses for all of us. That way, the junk will stop coming to my mailbox."

"Oh, let me fix it!" Stacy said. She reached down and grabbed the phone cord, and with one good, hard yank she pulled the cord out of the wall jack. At least the wires came out; the connector was still in the jack. "Now that problem is fixed," she said coldly.

"Fine with me. If I have to put up with this bullshit everyday, it's just as well." Problem solved, I thought, until I came home the next day and Shawn was back online.

"I thought your Mom ripped the cord out of the wall," I said.

"I found another cord."

"Does she know you're on line?"

"Yes, she told me I can get online, but you can't!"

"Listen, Shawn, I know damn well you're the one going into porn sites and causing all the junk mail, and I'm the one being accused. It's going to stop, or I'll take the computer down."

"Okay," he said. He didn't admit to it, but he didn't deny it either. It wouldn't matter much longer anyhow; the EBay auctions Stacy won had caused me to use most of the phone bill money, so I expected the phone would be cut off any day now.

It turned out to be the next day. I wondered why I hadn't received any calls at work since earlier in the day. When I came in the front door I was attacked by Stacy, Suzy, and Shawn because the phones didn't work. "What's wrong with the phones?" Stacy demanded accusingly.

"Nothing," I said.

"What do you mean 'nothing'? There's no dial tone."

"I figured that would happen. But as far as the phones go, they should be working fine if there was a dial tone—unless you've taken up throwing them again."

"You're a damn smartass! Didn't you pay the phone bill?" Stacy yelled.

"No, I didn't pay it, remember? I had to pay for all the EBay auctions you won."

"I can't believe you! You're an asshole, you know that?"

"Stacy, I *told* you I couldn't pay both the phone and light bill; it's cold outside and we need heat, so I paid the electric bill."

"So what are we supposed to do, sit around here all day without a phone?"

"Stacy, you *have* phones. They just don't work without dial tones. It'll be two weeks before I can afford to pay it, and I'll need to work overtime to do that. Next week the rent and lot rent payments are due, so it'll have to be the week after. Living paycheck to paycheck is hard. There *is* one other option—you could get a damn job and help me!"

Stacy didn't appreciate my poor attempt at humor in the least bit; the phone nearest her went flying across the room and hit the wall. Mobile home walls, as I found out, are not built as sturdily as those of apartments or houses, and they can't handle as much stress. The hole she'd just put in the wall provided the proof.

I sighed. "That was good, Stacy; I bet that phone learned its lesson."

"Screw you, bastard!"

Into the pocketbook she went, emptied the contents of the pill bottle into her hand, and took whatever amount of Xanax she had remaining. When she was done, she snapped at me, "Do you think your sorry ass can take me to the Emergency Room? I need Xanax."

"No, you don't. You just took at least two days worth; that's your problem, not mine."

"Well, then, I suggest you get on the phone with your doctor and tell him you need some. Tell him you lost yours."

"Stacy, I don't have any idea where my bottle is, or when the refills are due. You took all of mine; I haven't taken any in over a week."

"Then you won't be lying when you tell the doctor you lost your bottle, will you?"

"I'm not calling, sorry! My doctor *knows* better! He knows I can't go through that many pills in such a short amount of time."

"The only way he'd know is if you told him I was taking yours."

"I didn't tell him," I told her, "but I wouldn't put it past your previous psychiatrist to have told him."

"Why would he do that? I don't see him anymore, remember?"

"My doctor and your old one are partners in the same office. Don't you think they talk amongst themselves? If they put it in your file that you're always calling for refills on Friday nights, don't you think your new psychiatrist would know that? All he would need to do is request your records."

"Then you *have* to take me to the Emergency Room."

"No, I don't. You're a big girl. Take yourself."

Stacy did take herself to the ER, but I'd soon realize everything I'd seen so far was only the beginning of her violent tendencies. This was the tip of the iceberg, and there was a lot more getting ready to surface.

I came home a couple of days later and saw Shawn on the computer again. Stacy had gotten her Mother to pay the phone bill, and I was to pay her back the next week when I got paid—or at least that's what Stacy told me I was going to do. I knew that wasn't going to happen. There hadn't been any overtime, so I told her it would still be at least another week.

"You can't do that!" Stacy said, "I promised my Mom you'd pay her next week; she took it from her house payment money!"

"So you want me to take it from *my* house payment money? Is that what you're asking me to do?"

"I guess so," she said slowly.

"Well, your Mom should have cleared it with me before she gave you the money. You're the one who promised her, I didn't, and I *will* pay my rent on time. Don't even think about pulling the same stunt you did last time by taking the money out of the bank; I'll get a cashier's check and drop it in the box."

"So you're going to screw my Mother over like that?"

"No, I'm not, you are. You should have never made promises on my paychecks, Stacy."

"Well, I'm going to call her and tell her what you said."

"Okay, fine, I'll talk to her if she wants."

Stacy got her Mom on the phone, told her what I'd said, and handed the phone to me. Her Mother said without preamble, "Jonathan, I gave Stacy money from my house payment to pay your phone bill, and she said you'll pay me back next week. Now she says you're not!"

"I'm sorry, but I told Stacy you should have talked to me before you did that. My rent payment and lot rent is due next week also."

"Jonathan, why do you want to do an old lady like that?"

"Like what?"

"You're going to make me late on my house payment!"

"No I'm not, Stacy is. I've told you and her time and time again, I can't do this all alone, and it sure looks like she's not going to work to help me."

"Well, I won't help you anymore! You can bet on that!"

"Good. You can't take out more warrants on me if you don't give me money to help raise your daughter and grandkids. If we get kicked out of here like we have everywhere else, they can come to your house and live!"

"I should have never paid the damn thing! You could have sat over there for a year with no phone for all I care!"

"Fine by me!" I growled. "I never use the phone anyway. The only person who calls me is my Mom, and she can reach me at work. Cut the damn thing back off, I don't care."

I hung up the phone and walked into the bedroom. I'd just gotten home from work, and wanted to get my shoes off and sit down for a few minutes.

"Get back in here!" Stacy shouted. "I want to talk to you!"

"If you want to talk, you come in here!" I told her. I was tired of her ordering me around.

"You know, I hate your sorry ass!" she said when she came back into the bedroom. "I should have listened to my friends; none of them understood what I saw in you."

"You're talking about Jill, right? That's the only friend you have, to my knowledge. Next time you talk to her ask her what she told my Mom on the back deck the day we got married."

"What are you talking about?"

"Ask Jill! If she won't tell you, then ask my Mom, she may tell."

"I don't want to talk to your *Mommy!*" she said with disgust.

"And she doesn't want to talk to you either, but she won't lie to you."

"You're just trying to turn this around on Jill!"

"Yeah, you're right. I made it all up! I made it up to get even with you for your so-called imaginary affair!"

The next thing I knew I was showered with Pepsi. Stacy had thrown the contents of her glass onto me. "Goddammit!" I shouted. "You need help, Stacy, you need serious help!"

"You haven't seen anything yet!"

Now, that was a scary thought! I got up from the bed, took a clean, dry set of clothes into the bathroom, and took a shower to get the Pepsi out of my hair.

Between Stacy's insecurities, Shawn's secret porn-surfing and the enormous amount of junk mail resulting from his searches, the computer had really become a problem. I came home one afternoon and the bedroom door was shut. Stacy was nowhere to be seen.

I knew I shouldn't go back there and open that door; something told me there was going to be trouble. I wasn't going to be let down, either. There was trouble all right, big trouble.

The first thing that caught my eye was the computer table I'd spent an entire day putting together; it was laying on its side and broken in three pieces. The CPU was lying on the floor, the monitor was across the room, and the keyboard was in the window sill. Luckily, I hadn't bought a printer yet. Stacy was asleep. I didn't know what happened to cause all the damage, and to be honest I wasn't sure if I wanted to know.

The entire room was trashed. The farther into the room I walked, the worse it got. My dresser drawers had been taken out and turned upside down, spilling the contents into a big pile. There was shaving cream sprayed all over the bathroom mirror; from the looks of it after it had stopped dripping, it appeared she'd written 'asshole'. When I turned around and saw the other wall I noticed a very big hole in it. Anyone who's ever owned a mobile home will know that the walls are not drywall. The patterns that resemble wallpaper are part of the wall, making repairs nearly impossible if the manufacturer no longer uses that particular pattern.

I have no idea how many Xanax Stacy had taken, but she never knew I'd come into the room or gone back out. When Shawn came in the front door, I asked him what had happened, and he said he had no idea, as he and Suzy had been gone all afternoon. I went back to the bedroom to wake up Stacy, but she told me to leave her the hell alone. I picked up the phone to call her Mom, but the dial tone wasn't there. Now I had a pretty good idea that her Mom must have placed a stop payment on the check, and the phone service had been cut off again.

Shawn actually found it enjoyable to bring all his friends over to look at what his Mother had done to the bedroom. I was on my last nerve, and luckily had the next two days off.

I refused to clean up the mess. My thinking was that if the person responsible for the mess had to clean it up, maybe they'd decide it wasn't a good idea to do it again. As usual, I was wrong again! Shawn and I managed to get the computer desk pieces out of the bedroom and out the front door. The computer itself was put in the closet, but I had no idea if it still worked. As far as the big hole in the wall went, I was at a loss about what to do. My stress level was up, and I was a nervous wreck. I silently cursed myself for ever thinking about going to the store for Caramel Praline Crunch ice cream that time; there was no telling where my life would have ended up if I hadn't run into Stacy that night.

Stacy wasn't finished yet. She found it quite entertaining to open the closet door and slam it up against the corner of my chest of drawers, which knocked a hole in the closet door. She couldn't leave it as the small hole she'd produced. She stood there opening the door repeatedly until she'd knocked a very good size hole in the door. She wasn't satisfied until the corner of the chest of drawers had come through the other side of the door.

There was a small piece of wall separating part of the kitchen from the den area. This section of wall only went up about four feet from the floor, and had a section of stained glass window enclosure that went to the ceiling. At some point during dinner one evening, something was said that angered Stacy immensely; she threw her glass at the stained glass window and shattered it.

"What the hell did you do that for?" I asked.

"Leave me the hell alone!"

"I hope you're having fun destroying all this stuff. It's going to cost a considerable amount of money to repair, and I'll have no problem telling the owners who's responsible."

I began to remind Stacy of all the damage she'd done so far, in the hopes she'd see the error of her ways. I told her if the owners came over to visit, we'd be in trouble; there could possibly be legal action for destruction of property, and I wouldn't take the fall this time. When I mentioned the damage to the closet door she arose from the table, went into the bedroom, and continued pulling on the closet door until she was able to completely rip the hinges out of their bindings and the door came free. She carried it to the back door of the mobile home and threw it into the back yard.

"Now you don't have to worry about them seeing the hole in the door!" she shrieked.

My anxiety level rose even further when the mobile home owners called me at work on my first day back after my two-day break. "Jonathan, how are you?" the owner said politely.

"Um, not so good. Stacy is out of control with her medications."

"I've been trying to call, but I get a recording saying the phone is out of service."

"Yeah, I know. She won't work and I'm wearing myself down to exhaustion; I couldn't afford to pay the phone bill. I'm sorry."

"Jonathan, I like you and I know you're doing everything you can with no help; however, my wife and I think we need to come out tomorrow and see how the home looks. You understand, don't you?"

"Yes, I do understand. Please don't be in too much shock. I haven't done any of the damage; you'll see when you get there tomorrow."

When I informed Stacy as to the upcoming visit, she already had it figured out. With the exception of the window, the damage was concentrated in the bedroom.

She had Shawn go out, bring the closet door back into the home, and set it back in place. She then placed a decorative, long cloth calendar on the door to cover the hole. Her intentions were to be asleep, in pain, when they arrived. If they wanted to open the bedroom door and look inside, everything would appear normal—unless they actually came inside the room and turned around to see the large hole she'd knocked in the wall on her side of the bed.

When they arrived and the owner's wife came in, the first words out of her mouth were, "What happened to my stained glass window?"

Shawn and Stacy had already rehearsed this scenario. I don't remember what it was that Shawn said happened, but my expression and shaking my head told them otherwise. They looked in the kid's rooms and saw that everything was okay. Shawn proceeded to explain that Stacy was sleeping; she'd been up all night in enormous pain, he said. However, they were welcome to open the door and have a look inside, but should try not to wake her up if possible.

Just as Stacy had anticipated, they opened the door and everything appeared perfectly normal. They didn't walk inside to see the hole in the wall. As we talked, I could see the obvious disgust in the wife's face over her stained glass window. It seems she'd specifically requested it during the construction of the home. I told them, "All I can say is, just pick out a window of your choice, and

I'll pay for the glass and have it installed. Again, I'm terribly sorry. I have no control over Stacy's actions, and I want you to understand I'd never do anything like that."

"Yes, we know Jonathan," the wife said. "Both my husband and I know you're under a great deal of stress. It's only a window, which can be replaced. On our next visit, however, we'd like to have entry into the bedroom to look around."

"Yeah, I understand."

They left, and Stacy came out of the bedroom with a smile on her face. "Am I good, or what?" she said proudly.

"I'd have to guess on whose scale you're basing it on." I said, "If you're comparing yourself to the Devil himself, you're damn good; but I think you're mentally unbalanced and you really need to seek professional help. We've been married over seven years now, and I just don't know you anymore, Stacy. You've turned into a prescription drug junkie and you're going to be the death of me yet, just like your last husband."

It turned out that wasn't the best possible choice of words. I'd just turned to walk away, when both of her hands shoved me forward into the dishwasher.

Let the games begin!

14

Wake-Up Call

I'd made it through seven years of marriage to the She-Devil, and how I did it is still a mystery to me. I sometimes wonder if I'd broken a mirror and forgotten about it before I met Stacy; seven years of bad luck? I still had my sanity, thanks to my psychiatrists and therapists, but my body was beginning to show acute signs of distress.

It was July 2000, and I'd gone to my Mom's—for what I don't remember, nor do I remember the conversation I had with her that day. I do remember hearing a loud noise and coming back to reality. I'd left her house and turned the corner. I'd driven about a quarter of a mile, and hit a parked pickup; the sound of the impact is what brought me back to consciousness. Apparently, I'd blacked out sometime after turning the corner.

A neighbor sitting on his front porch told the police I started moving towards the right-hand side of the road and never tried to correct or apply the brakes. I must have been going less than 10 miles per hour, because the air bags didn't even deploy. The police officer was very nice, and so was the owner of the pickup. I wasn't ticketed, but the officer did notify the Division of Motor Vehicles that I might possibly have a medical condition. As a result, my psychiatrist had to fill out a form and send it to DMV stating he felt I was okay to drive daily. He explained that I was under extreme mental duress at the time, but that he was effectively treating me to correct the problem.

When I got home that day and told Stacy that I'd blacked out and had the accident, she seemed to be genuinely concerned. (I was wrong again, of course.) "What happened?" she asked.

"I'm not sure. I think I must have blacked out, and I hit a parked truck."

"So what are we supposed to do for a car now? I have medicine at the pharmacy that needs to be picked up; I'm going into withdrawals! Ain't this a bitch?"

"Stacy, I certainly appreciate your concern for me," I said sardonically, "but please try not to worry about it too much, okay?"

"What are you talking about?" she demanded.

"Is Xanax *all* you care about? I could have been seriously hurt, and the only thing on your mind is how we're going to pick up your medicine? You never once asked me if I was all right. The police officer showed more concern for my well being than you have."

"I'm sorry, it's just that I need my medicine!"

It didn't get any better. I wasn't sleeping very well, especially while working the 12-8 shift. I don't remember what night of the week it was, but I'd been up most of the day, and finally went to sleep about 6:00 p.m. one night in August. I overslept, and was driving a little faster than I should have been on my way to work that night when I topped the crest of a hill and spotted the police car sitting on the side of the road; he had me.

In September, while working 12-8, it happened again—same police officer, same place, about the same time, and the exact same speed. I hadn't been to court for the first ticket yet. I sat in the same paving company lot as the previous month while the officer wrote me another speeding ticket.

When the court date for the first ticket came, I asked the judge for permission to attend a defensive driving course. He agreed, and said he'd dismiss the ticket if I completed the class and mailed the certificate to the courts before a specified date. I made sure I completed the course before the court date for the second ticket, but waited to mail the form. When the court date for the second offense came, I pleaded guilty to the charge but told the judge I'd completed a driving class and offered to show him the certificate of completion. I thought I was going to get away with it until the clerk sitting next to the judge said, "That's on another driving offense, Your Honor!"

Damn! Almost pulled it off, I thought.

During the month of November, while I was working the 12-8 shift, once again Stacy convinced me to take her to the Emergency Room, this time at about 9:00 p.m. I called a co-worker who drove past the hospital on his way to work, and asked if he'd pick me up on his way. He said he'd pick me up at 11:30 outside the ER. Stacy and Shawn, who'd recently gotten his license, could drive the car home; I'd find a ride home in the morning.

I received a phone call at 2:30 that morning at work; I thought it would be Stacy telling me she'd made it home okay, but was surprised when the co-worker who'd answered said it was a police officer. I answered the phone not knowing what to expect.

"Mr. David, this is Officer Harris with the County Police. Your wife and stepson have been involved in an accident. They're okay; I'm at the hospital now. Can you come here?"

"Um, no, I had to get a ride to work this evening. Someone picked me up from the hospital; I left her in the Emergency Room."

"Yes, that's what the doctor said. He'd sent her home, and the accident happened on the way."

"You said they're okay?" I asked.

"They're shaken up, but they're okay."

"What happened?"

"Your stepson was driving when another vehicle ran a stop sign and T-boned the car containing your wife and stepson. The force of the impact pushed the car into a ditch, causing it to flip over on its roof, and then pushed it up a small embankment. Your wife had to be cut out of the car, sir. She's asking for you to come here."

"Officer, I don't have a way!"

"You're about three miles away, aren't you?"

"Yessir."

"Okay, I'll come and get you—but you'll have to find a way back to work if you need to return."

"That'll be fine," I said, relieved.

"I'll be there in ten minutes."

My boss was reluctant to let me to leave. They'd heard all the horror stories about Stacy, and thought this was just another of her scams. However, the co-worker who'd answered the phone verified that I did receive the call, and that it was a police officer who'd called.

True to his word, a police car arrived to pick me up about 10 minutes later. On the ride to the hospital, the officer told me the other driver had fallen asleep, run through a stop sign, and broadsided my car at what they estimated to be over 60 miles per hour—there were no skid marks. He elaborated further by saying that the passenger seat in which Stacy was sitting had become completely dislodged, and was in the back seat. Stacy was found upside down in the seat, and had to be cut out of the car. He said the car was a total loss. Ironically, Officer Harris was the very officer who'd written me two speeding tickets in the paving company's driveway in August and September. The other road where the driver ran the stop sign intersected the road I normally took at the bottom of the hill, about twenty feet from the paving company's driveway. He told me he'd been sitting in his usual spot at the crest of the hill when the accident occurred. He didn't remember me personally, or writing the tickets, but he *did* recognize the car.

When I got to the ER, I found that the accident had knocked out all of Stacy's front teeth, and there was damage to her back, legs, and arms. Shawn and the other driver were shaken up, but there were no signs of broken bones or major damage. Just my luck the other driver was operating with a suspended license and had no car insurance. The doctor said both Stacy and Shawn would be held overnight for observation. I called my Dad at 3:00 in the morning, and he wasn't thrilled, but he drove twenty miles to take me the three miles back to work. My co-worker dropped me off at the hospital after I left work that morning.

I believe it was Stacy's oldest son who came to the hospital that morning and took us home, but I can't be absolutely sure; I was barely hanging by a thread at that point. I couldn't take any more stress. When I saw the car later that morning, I was amazed either of them had survived; the only pieces of equipment salvageable on the car were the taillights.

I was barely clinging to my sanity at this point, and Stacy's demeanor had now become much worse due to the pain from the accident. It didn't take her long to go through all the medicine she'd been prescribed by the ER doctor, which only caused her to became even more violent and mean. She'd sit on the edge of the bed, and by flinging her feet she'd knock more holes in the wall while she cried and cursed.

"Why is God doing this to me?" she'd say. "Am I a bad person, Jonathan?"

As much as I wanted to say she was a spawn of Satan, I didn't. I opted out by saying everything happens for a reason. I didn't tell her I thought she was being punished for the way she'd treated me; I didn't think she'd appreciate my remarks very much. She sat on the edge of the bed every day, and continued to kick the wall until she'd knocked out a section of wall about the size of a small piece of plywood.

Things were rapidly plunging from bad to worse. My car insurance company paid off the Firebird and provided me with a rental car for two weeks. I went back to Old Faithful, the credit union, about buying a new car; I wanted to purchase another Firebird. However, I was told that wasn't going to happen—they wouldn't get suckered twice. The last car loan had gone through on the premise that I couldn't/wouldn't be around Stacy for two years, but I hadn't upheld my end of the bargain. I can't say I blamed the loan officer. Of course she didn't say it, but I knew by her face that she was disgusted with me. She understood I had to work and I needed transportation to get there; so, in all actuality, she was doing me a huge favor. She agreed to loan me money to purchase another car, but only for the balance I'd owed on the loan the insurance company had just paid off. I wasn't in a position to haggle. I had no choice but to take their offer for the same amount the insurance company had paid off. I wasn't able to get a Firebird, but I was able to purchase a 2001 Mustang.

I have a very sketchy memory of the events from the car accident in mid November until early January. I've tried to jog my memory, and have only remembered a few relevant facts of my life during this time.

I do remember that Stacy got angry about something once, and threw a small wooden table with knick-knacks on it into the bathtub. One of the table legs punctured a hole in the bottom of the tub, rendering it useless; the whole tub would have to be replaced. At some point during this timeframe the owners of the mobile home came by to do an inspection. Imagine their surprise when they walked into the bedroom and saw the closet door was gone, then turned around and saw half the wall was missing. I can't remember whether or not they saw the hole in the tub. Needless to say, they weren't sympathetic to Stacy's health at all; I'd anticipated that would happen. They knew I was nearing a breakdown and attempted to be civil towards me, but I knew what was coming. An eviction notice was imminent. I don't remember how soon after their inspection it arrived, but I know we had to be out of the home soon.

I remember one date: January 7, 2001. Stacy was out of Xanax—again. Her rotation between Emergency Rooms and other medical facilities put us at a Health Care Plus near my Mom's house that day. I remember having to go to a payphone located down the hall and around a corner to call my Mom to ask her to please bring me money for the co-payment. It was pitiful; I was forty-two years old and had to call my Mom for $10. I made between $50,000 and $60,000 a year at that time, but I had to live from paycheck to paycheck and never had any money. Where did it all go?

I've always heard a person should treat their body like a temple. Well, at that time, I surely wasn't worshipping mine. Looking back, I feel I was treating my body like an Interstate rest stop—just providing the essentials and moving on to another destination. I wasn't eating well, or getting near enough sleep. I worked any available overtime and there was always some form of crisis waiting for me at home. Neither Stacy nor the kids lifted a finger to clean the house; why should they? They knew I'd do it when I got home from work. I seemed to be the only one who couldn't stand to see a mess.

It wasn't uncommon for me to come home after sixteen hours and find Shawn and Suzy sitting on the couch watching television. Stacy would be holed up in the bedroom cursing God and kicking out wall panels. Yet they would wait for me to get home and ask, "What's for dinner?"

On that fateful Sunday, January 7, I'd no sooner gotten back to the waiting room from calling my Mom when Stacy asked me to go back to the payphone and call Suzy to let her know where we were. I remember dialing the phone number Stacy had given me, but I must have dialed somewhere into the Twilight Zone—because I woke up in the Emergency Room of the nearest hospital. I often tell people that the man upstairs was watching out for me that day. What better place to collapse than a health care facility, which happened to be located next door to the rescue squad?

My doctor said it best when he noted that my body was in dire need of help. My brain state needed my body to survive, so to protect me, my brain shut me down. The doctor told me to think of the blackout as an early warning signal.

Of course, I have absolutely no memory of anything after dialing the phone number. My parents told me of the events that happened afterwards. My Mom had come to the facility to bring me the co-payment money, but saw only Stacy in the waiting room. Stacy told her I was at the payphone down the hall. Mom walked halfway down and didn't see me, so she went back and told Stacy. Stacy told her the phone was around a corner, so my Mom went back, turned the corner, and saw me lying on the floor, gasping for breath. She ran back to the front desk and quickly got help. My Mom told me I fought the male nurse trying to get me into a wheelchair; for some reason, I kept crossing my legs.

Apparently, after dialing the number I blacked out and fell to the floor, landing on my left shoulder and the left side of my head.

They'd put me in a bed at the medical facility to get my breathing and vital signs under control while waiting for the rescue squad to arrive. My Mom had called my Dad, so he was on the way. When Dad arrived, my Mom told him how Stacy had immediately gone into action as an actress, playing the role of a loving, concerned wife.

When he and Mom came back to the room I was in, Dad wasted no time in informing the doctor that Stacy had caused my breakdown through the never-ending stress she'd kept me under—and for good measure, Dad put in his two cents about her Xanax addiction. He took his ranting one step further by explaining that Stacy had already caused one husband to die, and now she was working on me.

"So you don't think your son took an overdose of Xanax, which caused his collapse?" the doctor asked. In a roundabout way, without betraying patient confidentiality, the doctor was indicating that Stacy had told her just that. Stacy was shifting the blame to me—again.

"Hell, no!" Dad replied. "But I wouldn't put it past her to *say* that he did, so you'd give her more. This is just a game with her. She goes to all the Emergency Rooms in the area trying to get pills."

While the rescue squad personnel were preparing me for the ride to the hospital, the doctor looked at Stacy's chart and realized she was a damned good actress. She admitted to my Dad that she'd been taken in by Stacy's performance, and had indeed given Stacy a prescription for Xanax. The good doctor then informed my parents that she'd made an entry into Stacy's chart, stating she was not to be given any narcotic drugs under any circumstances on further visits.

When I came back to consciousness, I had no idea where I was, how I'd gotten there, or even what had happened. My parents were sitting next to the bed, and told me I was in the Emergency Room of the local hospital. I was being monitored for possible head trauma; I had been mumbling and talking incoherently since I'd come back to reality. I tried to adjust my position in the bed, but the searing pain I felt shooting through my left shoulder told me there was definitely some damage there. My Mom tried to explain everything that had taken place. "I found you lying on the floor; you were gasping for breath," she said. "There's no telling how long you were lying there before I found you."

"Where was Stacy?" I asked.

"I don't really know. She never left her seat during the whole ordeal—she was probably scared she'd miss them calling her name to see the doctor. Jonathan, are you aware you could have *died* lying there on that floor?"

I looked away. "I guess you're right," I admitted.

"I told the doctor at the health care facility what was going on!" my Dad said forcefully. "She said she'd already written the bitch a prescription, but it would be the last she'd get from *that* place."

"What's wrong with my shoulder?" I asked. "It hurts really bad."

"You fell on it, I'm sure." my Mom said. "When I found you, you were lying on your left side, so it's probably bruised. Are you listening to what I'm saying? You could have *died!* Stacy was more concerned about her Xanax than you. She never once checked on you. She said you'd been gone for over fifteen minutes when I arrived."

"They need to X-ray my shoulder," I gasped.

"The doctor is concerned you might have a head injury," Mom said. "You may have a concussion. There's a pretty nasty bump on your head from hitting the floor."

"Did they say when I can leave here?"

"They'll be keeping you overnight for observation, honey," Mom said, gently. "You may have had a stroke."

Just then, the ER doctor came in and said my room was ready, and they'd be transporting me upstairs soon. If my sketchy memory serves me right, I'd just received yet another sign that someone high above was indeed looking out for me. The only room they had available was on the third floor, in the surgical unit. I'd need that room in a couple of days, as I'd soon learn. The ER doctor also said they'd be taking a shoulder X-ray first thing in the morning; I guess they'd heard enough of my whining about it hurting so badly.

Once I was settled in my room, my parents went home and I went to sleep. I woke up sometime during the night and wanted to know what time it was, so I got out of the bed and walked to the nurse's station—but no one was there. I was bending down to look at the time on a computer monitor when a nurse caught me and called Security. I explained I only wanted to know the time, and went back to my room.

Early the next morning, Monday, the radiology department came and wheeled me to X-ray for a brief series of films. I'd been back in my room about an hour when a foreign doctor came in and introduced himself. He said he'd reviewed the X-rays, and the news was not good at all. The impact of my dead weight falling onto the concrete floor had caused the ball of my shoulder to shatter into three pieces. Surgery was imminent, and if it wasn't successful, I'd need a complete shoulder replacement. The surgery was scheduled for Wednesday, he said.

"We need to load you up on antibiotics and allow time for the swelling to recede a little first," Dr. Syriana told me.

"But it can be repaired, right?" I asked.

"Mr. David, I'm not going to tell you it's an easy procedure; it's not. I can probably get the ball back together, but the problem is blood flow to the bones afterwards. If it takes, you'll probably be okay, but if the bones don't get an ample blood supply after surgery, you'll need a replacement."

"So if it takes the blood flow okay, my shoulder will be good as new?"

"I wish I could tell you it was that simple, Mr. David, but you have a very serious break and you'll probably never get more than 50% use of your left arm after this is over. And it will take many months of physical therapy to get that much use; it will be a long and painful process. I'm sorry."

"I understand. Thanks for being honest."

He glanced down at my chart. "Are you currently seeing a psychiatrist?" he asked.

"I haven't seen one in about a year now. Why?"

"Because this is a heavy burden to carry, I've talked to your parents, and they've filled me in on your situation. I'll have someone come and talk to you, okay?"

"That'll be fine."

"Okay, I'll see you Wednesday morning, then," Dr. Syriana said brightly, and left the room.

My parents arrived a few minutes after he'd left and I tried to explain what the doctor had said—but they already knew. "You're going to have a couple of visitors in a little while," my Dad warned.

"Who? I don't think I'm up to seeing Stacy right now."

"It's not Stacy. Have you even heard from her?"

"Not a word."

"She's busy packing and getting out of the mobile home," my Mom said. "We talked to the Mencinos this morning."

"Oh shit, I forgot about the eviction notice!"

"Well, don't you worry about it," Dad said. "You didn't do the damage, and the Mencinos know that. They're the ones coming to see you, Jonathan."

"Why did you tell them it was okay? I don't think I can face them right now!"

Mom said, "They're not upset with you, son; it's Stacy they're holding responsible. They like you, and were very concerned when we told them what had happened. They wanted to come see you, and we told them it would be okay. I think it may be good for your state of mind to hear it from them. That'll be one less thing you have to worry about right now. You look really bad, Jonathan—Stacy almost killed you this time. I hope you'll consider this as a sign, and get away from that woman."

"So how long do you think I'll be in here?" I asked weakly.

"Your surgery is Wednesday, and from what the surgeon is saying, it's not going to be a picnic," Dad said. "I'd say you'll probably be here at least a week."

"Dammit, what about work?"

"I've taken care of that. You're on a Medical Leave of Absence. Now, is there something we can bring you from home, maybe a book or some magazines?"

"No, I can watch the TV. I don't feel like reading right now. Besides, they put me on pain medicine for my shoulder, and I couldn't concentrate anyway. But can you get me something cold to drink?"

"Sure. Like what?"

"A Dr. Pepper would be good, with lots of ice. All they have here is caffeine-free Coke and ginger ale."

"I'll run down to the cafeteria," Mom said, and left the room.

About 10 minutes later I heard my Mom talking to someone as she came down the hallway towards my room; she entered with the Mencinos following.

"Hey, Jonathan, how are you feeling?" Mr. Mencino asked heartily.

"I'm okay, considering the circumstances. Um . . . I'm really sorry about . . ."

"Jonathan!" Mrs. Mencino broke in. "Let's not talk about the house, okay?"

"Yes, ma'am. I just feel so bad . . ."

"We know you didn't cause any of the damage; we know it was all Stacy, and you tried to tell us that on numerous occasions. It can be repaired," Mr. Mencino said.

"But there's so much damage, it's going to cost a lot of money! The bathtub, the wall, and all the other stuff she damaged . . ."

"We've got it all under control, Jonathan. However, there *is* one thing I was hoping you could explain."

"I'll try."

"What happened to the skylight in the kitchen? There's something all over it."

I sighed. "Back in July or August, I don't remember which month, Stacy got in one of her bitchy moods because it was so hot inside and the air conditioner couldn't keep up. Between her and Shawn, they came up with the idea of putting a dark green plastic trash bag up inside the skylight to keep the sunlight out. Instead of stretching it across the opening and using thumb tacks, Shawn found a glue stick and drew all over the skylight and shoved the bag inside the recessed area. It didn't stay up there very long . . . but the sun beating down on the light caused the glue to permanently become part of the skylight itself."

"That boy's a real genius, isn't he?" my Dad said sarcastically.

"We got an estimate and it's not as bad as we thought," Mr. Mencino said. "We'll use drywall to replace the wall she kicked out, and then wallpaper the whole room. Of course, the bathtub, skylight, bedroom and closet doors, and the stained glass window have to be replaced, but the manufacturer has those items. With labor it comes to almost $7,000. However, I have a friend who says he can do it for less. I'll have the total I need to collect from you and Stacy by the time we go to court."

"He'll pay his share!" Mom piped up. "Jonathan has *always* paid his debts."

"We're not worried about that, Mrs. David," Mrs. Mencino said. "He's a good guy and we like him a lot."

"Can't say the same for that wife of his, though," Mr. Mencino said darkly.

Thankfully, a nurse walked into the room just then and said she'd be back in a few minutes to take my vital signs, and that she'd then be starting an IV to load me up with antibiotics. I was glad for the interruption. I did feel more confident about the Mencinos and appreciated their visit, but I was scared that things were going to get out of hand if the discussion turned to Stacy and her escapades. Visiting hours were almost over anyway, and everyone seemed to be preparing to leave for the night.

I was formulating a plan in my head, and as soon as everyone left I could put it into motion. I knew that once an IV was started, I would be confined to my room. As of now, I could roam freely to the bathroom; so I needed to make one last attempt at escape before the ball and chain were attached.

I hadn't had a cigarette since sometime on Sunday, and even though I was doing well, the thought of taking one last smoke was downright appealing—and I couldn't get the thought out of my head. I knew that shift change for the nurses would be the best time, but that was two hours away. I knew if the nurses followed the same schedules I did as far as work went, they had certain things they'd do at certain times each shift. I'm sure they'd make one last run-through with their patients before calling it a night's work. Putting in my IV was on the schedule for my nurse's last run, so I had to go now.

I got out of the bed and checked the hallway in both directions; no one was in sight. The bank of elevators was down the hall to my left, about 20 yards away. I quickly walked out of my room, went down the hall, and pushed the 'down' button, hoping like hell the elevator was there—but it wasn't. I had no choice but to get back to my room quickly and stand at my door until I heard the familiar 'ding' informing me the elevator had arrived at my floor. I heard the ding and, looking both ways, saw that the coast was clear. The elevator doors were opening as I approached. Much to my delight, it was empty and I turned to get inside.

"Hey!" a voice hollered.

I turned to see the same Oriental nurse who'd caught me earlier looking at me, but it was too late to stop now. I stepped inside and pushed the button for the first floor. I don't know if she came towards the elevator or not, but the doors closed, and I was on my way. I knew the hospital's front doors were locked after visiting hours were over, so I headed to the Emergency Room entrance. I was almost home free, and then I only needed someone to be outside smoking to get a cigarette for myself. As I approached the ER, the wooden doors were closed, but that wasn't a big deal; they usually were, to keep the rest of the hospital isolated from the ER. I'd spent many a night at this ER with Stacy and her Xanax habits. The psychiatric floor I'd been on just a little over a year before, the one I was in when Stacy called and said I was going to kill the whole family, was on the fifth floor. I knew my way around the hospital.

As I approached the wooden door, I put my arm out to push it open, but the very courteous security guard had seen me coming and opened it for me.

"Where are you going?" the guard asked. "Out to get a smoke?"

"Yes," I answered.

"Well, I just received a phone call, and they're requesting your presence back on the third floor," he said, grinning at me.

"Yeah, I know. I just wanted to get one last smoke in before they started the IVs and held me captive up there. As soon as I get a smoke, I'll go back."

I was hoping the guard would be sympathetic to my plight, but he wasn't. "I'm sorry, but I can't let you do that. I need to take you back to your floor." he said.

"Okay, I'll go back, I know the way."

"I know you do. I recognize you. I've seen you here often."

"Yeah, my wife comes here to get her prescriptions refilled at least twice a month."

"I thought so. Okay, let's go back upstairs."

He escorted me back to my floor, and the Oriental nurse was waiting with a scowl on her face. "Are you going to give me trouble while you're here?" she demanded.

"Probably," I admitted. "I'm not a very good patient, as you've probably noticed by now. At least upstairs on the fifth floor, they let me smoke every even hour."

"Well, I can arrange for you to go back up there if you'd like!"

"No thanks. I think I'll stay here."

"Good. Now get in the bed and I'll be back to start your IV."

She didn't take long to come back, pushing a cart with all kinds of torture devices on it. I hate needles, and the sight of one penetrating a body surface causes me to wince. I have to look away when given a shot. She thumped on my right hand until she was happy that she'd pissed the blood vessel off enough to get bigger, and said those famous words: "You're going to feel a little stick." I knew what was coming and looked away. I also knew she was going to put just a little extra 'stick' in it as punishment for trying to escape—which it categorically felt like she did.

Once the IV was in place, she played with the controls on the blue box on the IV pole and started the drip from the two bags hanging there. She pushed the pole back into the corner and moved the bed over to make it nearly impossible for me to get the pole out and walk around the room. She told me that if I needed to urinate I had to use the plastic bottle hooked onto a bed rail, and she left the room. I can only imagine what she told her relief at shift change. I knew they'd be keeping a close watch on me for the rest of the night.

Tuesday morning I received a visit from Dr. Kashadi, the psychiatrist Dr. Syriana had told me about. He was a nice guy, and seemed genuinely concerned. "Dr. Syriana has told me about your case and suggested I come to talk to you. It seems you've been through quite an ordeal."

"Yes, I've had a lot happening."

"Dr. Syriana is afraid you are being abused by your wife. Did she do the damage to your shoulder?"

"I guess you could say she did indirectly."

"Explain, please."

"She always keeps me stressed out. She abuses her medicine, and it seems my life is under constant turmoil. I was lucky I blacked out at a doctor's office."

"Why were you at the doctor's office?"

"So Stacy could get Xanax."

"Your wife's name is Stacy, then?"

"Yes."

"Ah, now I know who you are talking about. I have received calls from her about refilling her medicine. So if no one will refill over the phone, she goes to other doctors?"

"Yes. Other doctors, emergency rooms, urgent care facilities, etc."

"Has she ever hit you?"

"Well, yes," I said, looking away. I was ashamed to admit it. "She's only hit me a couple of times. She mostly throws things at me and threatens me a lot."

"Hmm. May I call you Jonathan?"

"Yes."

"Okay. Now, I don't mean to upset you, but it's okay, you can talk about these things freely with me. You're not alone, Jonathan.

There are many men who are abused, yet they do not speak of it. It does not make you any less of a man, okay?"

"Okay," I said glumly.

"Where is she now? Has she been to see you?"

"No she hasn't been here to see me. She's packing up the mobile home we live in. The owners were here last night to visit me, and they told Stacy to be out by Saturday."

"Mr. David, you're very lucky to have blacked out like you did. You could have had a heart attack or a stroke. Have they run tests to determine if you *did* have either of those?"

"I'm not sure. I think they said I didn't have a heart attack, but I'm not sure about having a stroke; but they may have said and I don't remember."

"I'll talk to your doctor and see," Dr. Kashadi said, soothingly. "Okay? Now, I'll come back to see you on Thursday. If there's anything you'd like to talk about, you let me know. Don't be ashamed to talk about it."

"Okay. I doubt I'll be remembering much of anything, though. They operate on my shoulder tomorrow, and I'll probably be out of it for a day or two."

"Are you worried about the operation?"

"Not really. I've heard lots of good things about Dr. Syriana. The nurses say if it can be fixed, he's the one to do it."

According to my parents, the surgery lasted for over 6 hours, but at the end the doctor told them it had gone well. He used titanium screws to put the ball of the shoulder back together, and used some type of wires to keep everything in place. He came to see me later that night, but I don't remember him doing so; the pain medication had me out of it for most of the day.

Thursday afternoon, a physical therapist came into the room, lifted my arm above my head a couple times, and said everything looked fine. Dr. Kashadi came back to visit, and asked me to call his office and schedule an appointment. He felt I really needed to talk to someone about the abuse issues.

Stacy finally showed up Thursday before my parents arrived. "How are you feeling?" she asked cheerfully.

"Okay, I guess," I growled. "Where the hell have you been? I've been here since Sunday, and you haven't even bothered to call!"

"Jonathan," she said with a smartass look on her face, "I have to pack the whole place up. We have to be out by Saturday, you know!"

I rolled my eyes. "You poor thing. Would you like to see if the doctor will let me go home now, so you can go back to bed and feel sorry for yourself? We wouldn't have to move if you could control your temper and stop destroying things."

"It seems to me the owners could give us more time, since you're hurt and I was in the car accident," she said tartly. "Why don't you call and ask?"

"Is that the only reason you came up here, Stacy? If it is, then carry your ass out of here. They already told me they wouldn't. This is all your fault anyway, for stressing me out so bad and causing me to fall."

"I didn't cause you to fall, and you know it!" she snapped.

"Oh yeah, I forgot. You told the doctor I took all your medicine, and *that's* what caused me to black out. Well, my Dad got him straightened out on that issue. If I were you I wouldn't go back there asking for any medication. It's been put in your chart now."

"Your Dad can go to hell!"

"You want me to ask him to save you a seat?"

She turned to leave, and ran into my Mom and Dad as they were coming into the room. Not a word was spoken between them. Stacy motioned for my Mom to come out into the hall. I later learned that she asked my Mom if I could go to their house when I was released from the hospital, since she wouldn't be able to take care of me, with her illnesses and all from the car accident.

She couldn't even leave the hospital without getting in the last word. According to the nursing supervisor, Stacy stopped at the information desk on the way out and made a report, one that prompted the nursing supervisor herself to visit my room.

"I'm sorry, but Mrs. David, his wife, made a report that you asked her to leave the room," the supervisor said, looking at my Dad.

"He did not!" I quickly spoke up.

"She just wants to start trouble. That's her way of playing games," my Dad said. "I wouldn't pay her any mind."

My Mother said, "She took me into the hall and asked if Jonathan could come to our house when he's released. There wasn't a single word spoken between Stacy and his Dad. It's a long story . . ."

"Okay, I understand; we just have to follow up on these things. I hope you understand I'm just doing my job."

"Yeah, it's not a problem," my Dad said. "I'm used to her tactics."

I was released on Sunday and taken to my parents' home for what would be a very long and painful recovery.

15

Either She Leaves, or
Both of You Go!

When I arrived at my parent's home after my surgery, I was basically helpless. My hygiene skills were very limited, to say the least. I had to purchase an electric razor and a pair of loafers; tying my shoes was definitely not an option. Putting on a pair of pants was doable, but remarkably time-consuming, and putting on socks was even worse. My left arm was to remain in a sling until it was time to have the twenty-three staples removed at the surgeon's office. I was definitely *not* looking forward to that procedure—however, my concern was never justified, as it was almost painless, as I'd eventually find out. I felt nothing more than a pinch as each staple was removed.

After talking to Dr. Syriana, I learned the actual severity of my injury, and saw the X-rays for the first time. The surgeon was still very concerned about the blood supply to my shoulder bones, and he continued monitoring my condition with new X-rays every month to six weeks. He told me I'd be starting physical therapy in a couple of weeks, and my progress would be the ultimate judge of whether or not I'd ever be able to regain full use of my left arm.

As far as Stacy goes, much of my memory from this period is still very, very cloudy. After asking friends and family, I learned that Suzy was able to qualify for government subsidized housing this time, and that Stacy, Suzy and Shawn were living in an apartment about three miles away. I don't believe we had much contact at all during the first twelve months I was at my parents' recuperating . . .

at least, I don't remember any. It seemed as if she'd been erased from my mind.

I continued to see Dr. Kashadi on a bi-weekly basis, to keep my mental faculties as firmly in check as much as humanly possible after my ordeal.

I'd begun receiving medical disability checks from my employer, which amounted to about one-third of my normal salary. It barely paid my present bills, much less the past-due debts I'd accrued from Stacy's financial fiascos. All I could do was contact my creditors by telephone, and make arrangements to make reduced payments for my current debts. I had also requested a copy of my credit report, and tried to send a small sum each month to the creditors who were most severely damaging my credit status. With my Mom's help, we set up a monthly budget to begin the reparations. At least I took some solace in the fact that I was trying to make myself feel like a worthwhile person again.

There was still the matter of the Mencinos to deal with. They'd visited me at least three times while I was in the hospital, and I knew they were genuinely concerned about me as a person; but the damage to their mobile home still had to be repaired. I now understand how very naïve I'd been about issues with Stacy, but I certainly didn't expect the Mencinos to pay for Stacy's wrath against their property.

My parents and I met the Mencinos at a small coffeehouse near the courthouse to talk on the morning before my first, and hopefully last, court appearance to answer to the damage charges. Of course, as I should have expected, Stacy didn't show up—but she'd recently contracted an ambulance chaser to represent her interests in the car accident, and he showed up on her behalf.

The Mencinos' attorney, Mr. Brooks, apprised the judge of the damages to the home, which came to a total of $7,000. "Mr. David," the judge said, looking at me sternly, "do you dispute the amount of damages incurred to the mobile home that you and your wife resided in under a signed rental agreement?"

"No, Your Honor, I do not dispute the amount," I replied.

"Did you do any of this damage, sir?" the judge asked.

"No ma'am, it was all done by my wife," I said quietly, with my head down in shame. I fully expected a response from the ambulance chaser, but he said nothing.

"Your Honor," Mr. Brooks said, "my clients sympathize with Mr. David's situation, and have found someone who will repair the home for less as a favor to them. They are willing to take a lesser amount of $4,000."

She nodded. "Mr. David," the judge said, "it appears the Mencinos are willing to work with you on this. Since it was a joint contract, both you and your wife will be held equally responsible for the amount."

"That's fine with my client, Your Honor!" the ambulance chaser chimed in.

"Are you in agreement to paying the Mencinos $2,000?" the judge asked me.

"What if Stacy doesn't pay? Am I responsible for her share too?"

"The Mencinos are willing to draw up an agreement with Mrs. David's attorney," Mr. Brooks spoke up. "They'll place a lien on the settlement from the accident for her share of the damage."

"Well, this sounds like this is working out easily enough," the judge responded, "if Mrs. David's attorney is in agreement with your offer."

"That will be fine," he responded.

"Mr. David, do you have any further questions?" the judge asked me.

I was very surprised at the generosity of the Mencinos, and certainly didn't want to look the proverbial gift horse in the mouth, but there was something I had to say that I thought might not be well received. "Um, what about the deposit?" I asked, which had everyone looking at me with surprise.

"Your Honor, I'd like a minute to confer with my clients," Mr. Brooks told the judge. The looks aimed at me were not very hospitable; however, they'd already agreed to cut the amount $3,000, and I was in dire straits. I needed all the help I could get when dealing with the costs of Stacy's temper.

"Your Honor," Mr. Brooks said after a brief conference with his clients, "the Mencinos had neglected to mention the deposit, and agree that the amount now owed by the David's will be $3,000, or $1,500 apiece."

"Is that okay with your client?" the Judge asked the ambulance chaser.

"No problem, your honor!" he said quickly.

Of course he'd agree; I'd just saved Stacy $500. I'd wanted to ask if the entire $1,000 deposit could be deducted from my share, but I'd already pushed my luck once, and wasn't going to attempt it again.

"Is this agreeable to you, Mr. David?" the judge asked.

"Yes, Your Honor. I'll pay the $1,500 in full once I receive my income tax return."

"Fine. This case is settled, unless payments are not received—in which case the Mencinos are fully entitled to re-petition the court and place a judgment against the guilty party or parties. Is there any other business pertaining to this matter today?"

No one said anything, at which point the judge pronounced that the case was thereby considered settled.

I was scared to look the Mencinos in the eye after I'd pulled the trump card from my sleeve, but they seemed to be okay once we'd left the courtroom. We remained in contact after I'd paid my share, and I heard they received the money from Stacy's attorney about six months later. Last I heard, they'd sold the mobile home and moved out of state.

I'll never forget Stacy's attorney walking up to me in the vestibule of the courthouse afterwards and introducing himself. "That was pretty good, bringing up the deposit," he said slickly. "You caught them off guard."

I looked at him for a few seconds before I replied, "Well, I certainly didn't want to. They were being very generous towards me, but I have to pay all the bills now. My being on medical leave doesn't provide me enough money to do it all. Now, how do you expect to get a settlement on the accident when the guy had no car insurance?"

"Oh, we're suing your insurance company. You had uninsured motorist coverage, and we can sue up to the limits of it."

"Do I get any of this money?"

"No, the money goes to Stacy and her son."

"But it was *my* car! What about the amount of money I'd paid into it?"

"Was your loan paid off by the insurance company?" he asked. I admitted that it was, and he said, "Then the insurance company has settled their obligation towards you."

"That's not fair," I griped.

"It's the law. Mr. David. I'm sorry."

"So, what should I do now?" I asked the attorney.

"Do you really want my advice?"

"Yes, I need *some* kind of legal advice. I make too much money for a public defender, but I don't have enough to hire anyone right now."

"Okay, I'll give you my honest opinion. Get a divorce." He turned on his heel and walked away.

I had no idea, when I started, just how much of an ordeal physical therapy on my shoulder would be. I couldn't understand how not using my shoulder for six weeks could make it so stiff. I thought the muscles must have atrophied; but April, the physical therapist assigned to me, assured me that wasn't the case. "You've been through quite an ordeal. Your shoulder has basically been taken apart and put back together with a few new pieces. I'm not going to sugarcoat things by saying this will be easy. It's going to take months, and it will be very painful at times; but it can be done. You'll need to keep remembering that."

"And you think I can do this by coming here three times a week?" I asked. "Right now, I can move my forearm in and out, but my shoulder won't budge in any direction."

"It's going to take a lot of perseverance on your part. I'll show you the things we can do here, but there are also things you can do at home that will make your progress advance much faster."

"Okay, let's get started."

April had me lie on my back and raise both hands above my chest, forearms outstretched. She then placed a big red ball in my palms, and instructed me to move the ball backwards towards my head the best I could.

After a week of working at home on this therapy, I was able to get almost a five-degree range of motion from the shoulder joint. I went through the same routine each and every visit, doing workouts on various machines. Each visit ended with April measuring the degree of movement I'd achieved.

I'd really begun to enjoy my monthly visits to Dr. Syriana; he was a likeable man with a terrific attitude, not to mention the fact that I recognized he'd done a remarkable job on putting me back together. "So, how are you doing, my good friend?" he'd always say on each visit.

"I'm getting there, Doc!" I'd always reply.

We'd go through the usual X-ray procedure, and he'd evaluate the blood supply to the ball of the shoulder. "Everything looks good, my friend! You are progressing nicely with therapy?" he'd ask.

"Yes. It hurts and almost brings tears to my eyes sometimes, but April is very good to work with, and I feel I'm making good progress."

Every other visit I'd get a shot of cortisone, which stung like hell, but did ease the pain quite a bit.

Before the beginning of May, I was able to drive myself the two miles to therapy. Even though my left arm's movements were still very restricted, I could hold the wheel steady while switching gears with my right arm. I don't know what Stacy was doing for transportation, because I'd had my car since coming to my parents' in January. I'm sure her Mom had done something to help them. She always did.

At the end of May, I went to Dr. Syriana's office in good spirits. The last measurements April had taken showed that I'd achieved forty percent use of my shoulder now. I thought he'd share in my optimism, but he was cautious in his assessment. "I agree you've made remarkable progress over the last three months, my friend," he told me. "However, I'm afraid you may never get more than seventy percent use of your shoulder. I just want you to understand that."

"But I don't think I'll be permitted to go back to work under those circumstances, Doc!"

"I have the sheet here from your employer, and they say you must be able to lift forty pounds over your head and place it onto a shelf. Do you feel you will be able to do this?"

"I'm damn sure going to try!"

"I admire your determination, friend, and I hope you will, but let me be frank: when I finished the operation, I would have bet my paycheck you'd never work again. I really think at the end of June, you should consider applying for full-time disability."

I thought I was doing so well, and had been excited at my progress—and the good doctor had just let all the air out of my balloon. I decided then and there that I'd show him I could do it. I began even more frequent and more strenuous exercises at home. I'd lie in the bed at night and raise my left arm straight up, and by using my right arm as a brace, I'd slowly push, despite the pain, until I was able to touch the wall behind the bed with my left hand. I'd repeat this procedure nightly, until I was able to touch the wall without the aid of my right arm. I'd then slide farther down in the bed and repeat the same procedure with both arms until I'd achieved my goal.

April saw the effects my home exercises were having, and was very impressed with the progress I'd made after a month's time. By the time I went to see Dr. Syriana at the end of June I'd achieved the seventy percent he thought neither of us would ever see. "Your X-rays look good, my friend!" he told me. "You're doing really well. I've instructed April to start working on your ability to lift the forty pounds. Are you up to it?"

"Yes, I'm ready, Doc. My disability pay ends at the end of July, and I have to be back at work by then—or I'm going to fall into that sinkhole called debt!"

The doctor was almost right. It had been painful for sure to get to seventy percent usage, but moving forward was a very slow process. I wearily took the Doc's advice, called Social Security to ask about applying for disability, and was advised they would send me the application by mail. When it arrived, I looked at everything it entailed and decided it was too much trouble; I'd never been a quitter, and wasn't going to start now. I was now barely able to lift the tray of forty pounds over my head and place it on a shelf, but I could do it. The problem was, my right arm had to go higher to account for the slant from my weaker left shoulder.

At the end of July, my therapy sessions were over, at the insistence of my insurance company; they weren't going to pay for it any longer. I made my last scheduled visit to Dr. Syriana's with the news that I'd achieved seventy-eight percent usage of my left arm.

"That's probably all you're going to get, my friend," he cautioned me. "I'm going to release you to return to work, but it is up to your employer to determine whether you meet their expectations. Did you apply for disability?"

"I called and asked about it and I received the paperwork, but it just looked so complicated and I'm not a quitter, so I haven't done anything with the papers yet," I admitted.

"Well, I'll give you another cortisone shot and wish you the best. When will you try to go back?"

"I made an appointment for Monday morning with the medical department at work, to see if I can clear through."

"Good luck, my friend, and keep me posted. Call the office if you need to see me."

I went in that Monday morning full of hope, but my employer's physician didn't like the fact that I couldn't lift the forty pounds evenly, so my request to return was a washout. I went back home heartbroken, but I kept at it. After ten days, I made another appointment and tried again. They agreed to let me return the next day, but only because my boss had said he could keep me inside for a week or two to let me acclimate myself back to the job. I did fine on my first day back; in fact, I worked sixteen hours each that Friday and Saturday. I worked my normal shift on Sunday, so I was able to get my forty hours in three days. I kept working and exercising diligently, and by the end of September, I stopped by physical therapy one afternoon and had April measure my usage. I'd made it to ninety-two percent—I knew I could do it!

I jumped into work at full speed, and finished the year with a decent income for having only worked a little over four months; I'd put in a lot of overtime. My bills were all up to date and I'd made considerable progress on my credit report. As far as I remember at this time, I spent the entire eighth year of my marriage to Stacy with very little, if any, contact with her. I don't believe Stacy played an active part in my life until March of the next year, 2002.

During the fifteen-plus months while I was staying at my parents', Stacy, Suzy, and Shawn were still living in Suzy's apartment. Shawn had developed the attitude that he was above the law and was constantly testing his theory; thus, he was always in some sort of trouble. Suzy had the attitude that it was her world, and we should all be thankful she allowed us to live in it. I guess the old adage 'the apple doesn't fall far from the tree' fit perfectly; Stacy had allowed them to grow up to be just like her. Stacy and Suzy were always at each others' throats; they couldn't get along for thirty minutes. Shawn and his girlfriend had taken off one night in the girlfriend's Mom's car; of course they'd taken it without permission, which prompted both teens to be considered runaways in a stolen vehicle. They were eventually apprehended three states away, when they ran out of money and called Suzy's apartment. It seems nothing had changed for the better in Stacy's life during my fifteen month hiatus.

However, I'd decided it was time for me to move forward and better myself; I wanted to move into my own place. So I signed a lease on an apartment—and Stacy somehow convinced me to allow her to move in. To this day, I'm not sure how she talked me into it. I remember telling her, "Stacy, I don't know if we're going to make it! I can't live with your kids anymore, and I only signed for a one-bedroom apartment."

"Jonny, I can't live with them either! Why do you think I want to move in with you? We *are* still married, you know; it's been almost nine years, and we'll finally have the chance to be alone!"

"I just don't know," I said reluctantly. "A lot of damage has been done, in more ways than one. I don't want anything to do with Suzy or Shawn. I'm sorry for feeling that way, but that's the way it has to be."

"Suzy and Shawn are staying in the apartment they're in now," she declared. "They'll be fine."

I let her convince me. Like an idiot, I called the apartment manager and added Stacy's name to the lease the day before I moved in.

Shawn had met a girl online and took off across the country by train to visit her. A month before he left on his 'See America by Rail' excursion, he'd decided he was going to be a fireman, and finally found a fire department willing to let him volunteer. He had a fit until he finally got the uniform. He wore it day in, day out every single day. He'd walk around the malls trying his best to look important. He'd been ticketed frequently by police for parking in fire lanes while he performed his own fire inspections of local businesses, yet he never bothered to pay the tickets or attend his court dates. We would find out after he'd gone that the police were looking for him; a *capias*, a kind of civil warrant, had been issued for his arrest.

Suzy realized, after Stacy was gone, that she had to fix her own glass of Pepsi if she wanted it done—and if something required getting off the couch, it was a problem for Suzy. Worse, she had to fix her own meals and clean up after herself now that Stacy wasn't there to cook, clean, and wait on her hand-and-foot. Life was so hard! We'd been in the apartment for a week when Suzy came knocking on the door. "Mom," she whined, "can I stay here for a few days? It's lonely with Shawn gone."

"No!" I said very quickly. "There's only one bedroom, and I know how you are."

"I'm not asking *you*," Suzy sneered. "I'm asking my Mom."

"And I'm answering for your Mom. The answer is no!"

"My Mom's name is on the lease here, so *she* can make the decision!" Suzy shouted.

"Your Mom is listed as an *occupant*. My name is on the lease, and I said no!"

Suzy stormed out the door, slamming it behind her, and of course I was in trouble.

"You could have agreed to let her stay just one night, you know," my wife pouted. "What would it hurt? I'll make it up to you if you agree to let her stay just one night, Jonny."

And so the games began again. I agreed to the one night, and Suzy came back with a smirk on her face, as if to say "I showed you, didn't I?'

One day turned to two, then three, and Suzy knew exactly what she was doing. She'd decided she knew the law very well, in fact, and was going to become a lawyer. She was planning to exercise her legal rights by saying she'd spent "X" amount of nights there, and couldn't be put out without a proper eviction notice, thereby giving her 30 more days. I nipped that one in bud by visiting the apartment manager's office, and made him aware of the situation that was slowly being formulated by the legal prodigy visiting our apartment. He took care of it the next day. He came with the maintenance workers to inspect the air conditioning filters, and saw Suzy sprawled out on the couch, as usual.

"I hear you've been staying here for a few days," he told her briskly, "and I'm informing you now that you can't spend more than two nights a month here as a guest. This is a one bedroom apartment, and there's only room here for two occupants."

With a smirk on her face, Suzy sneered, "You can't make me leave without an eviction notice; I've been here three days, and I know the law!"

The manager rolled his eyes. "That's what you think, kid. If you're here tomorrow when I come back, I'll call the law, and you can take it up with them after they escort you out of here. I don't care what you *think* you know, I know what this lease says, and you're not a part of it."

After the manager left, Suzy had quite a few choice words for me—and Stacy did nothing to shut her up. I saw firsthand that blood is thicker than water. When she was done, Stacy turned on me. "Did you go to the manager?" she asked, eyes blazing.

"Yes, I did."

"And why did you do that?"

"To get her out of here!" I declared. "I told you from the beginning this wasn't a good idea. She has her own apartment, and she can go there."

"But why did you go to the manager? Why didn't you tell her yourself?"

"You think it would have mattered? Stacy, the only way I can get her out of here is to physically throw her out, and I'm not going to put a hand on her and get arrested for assault. You won't stand up for yourself because you're scared of her. Well, I'm not. I've got enough sense to do things the legal way this time."

"I just wish you hadn't involved the manager. You've only made things harder for me!"

"Stacy, you're welcome to leave with her if you don't like the way I'm doing things. My name is on this lease, and I told you I'm not living with your kids. Period. It's your choice, but one of you is leaving today—and I know which one that is."

I won that battle, and Suzy rode out of the apartment on her bottom lip. Stacy was upset with me for standing up to her and Suzy, but I didn't care. They'd been out of my life for over a year and I'd managed to stay alive; I could do it again. Stacy decided to stay, but she pouted about it for a few days before she got over it—for the time being.

Shawn came back from his trip late one Monday night, and Stacy agreed to let him stay at the apartment for one night, since I was working the midnight shift. I went by my parents' house that Tuesday morning before going to my apartment. We were sitting on the front porch drinking a cup of coffee when their phone rang. It was Stacy.

"What are you doing over there?" she demanded.

Perplexed, I said, "I stopped by on my way home. Why?"

"You need to come home right now!"

"Why? What's wrong?"

"The police have been here looking for Shawn. Get home now!"

As I drove home, I wondered what the stupid kid had done this time. I noticed a couple of police cruisers sitting in the parking lot of the apartment complex as I parked and went to my apartment.

Stacy met me at the door, furious. "Did you call the police and tell them Shawn was home?"

"Hell no. Why?"

"Well, somebody did, and they've been here already!"

"Maybe they're just doing their job," I told her. "Anyway, they're sitting in the parking lot. Where is he now?"

"He snuck out after they came the first time," Stacy said sullenly . . . which indicated to me that she'd lied to the police and covered for her juvenile delinquent son.

A knock at the door interrupted our conversation. It turned out the police hadn't believed Stacy's denials that she hadn't seen Shawn; the officers in the parking lot had been waiting for another officer to arrive with a search warrant. I answered the door and explained that I'd been at work all night, and Stacy had told me Shawn had left. When they produced the search warrant, I had no problems with them coming inside—but Stacy did. Not long after, they found Shawn crouched in the corner of a closet. Stacy tried to act convincing when she told the officers that she didn't know he'd come back, and she was completely unaware he was in the closet.

Whether they believed her or not, Shawn was handcuffed and taken away. Of course, if I planned to get any sleep that day, I'd have to take Stacy to the police station to see what all this ruckus was about first. I admit I wasn't taken by surprise when Stacy was called into the Magistrate's office and charged with obstruction of justice. I knew from the tone of her voice when they found him that she had lied to the police and me; he was in the closet the whole time. I didn't believe her acting, and obviously, neither did the police—or the judge.

At that point Shawn's budding criminal career was in its early stages, so he was sent off to juvenile detention for ten days for numerous parking violations, impersonating a fire department official, and failure to appear in court.

Things didn't get any better after that, even though Stacy and I were supposedly 'alone' in the apartment. I should have known better from the beginning—but as always, I gave her the benefit of the doubt, and walked away with mud on my face again.

I don't remember the exact cause of the argument, but eventually Stacy and I had a big one. She stormed out of the apartment one September morning and sat in the parking lot of the complex, blowing the car horn and revving the engine. Her actions obviously bothered the other tenants that early in the morning, which resulted in a few noise complaints to the office manager. I knew it was trouble when I saw the manager's number on the Caller ID. He asked me to please come to the office at my earliest convenience. Of course, being nervous as hell from my past experiences, I went right away. I felt like a child being called to the principal's office.

He got right to the point. "Mr. David, we have a problem with your wife's actions this morning. We've received a few previous complaints about her slamming doors and yelling, but this morning's escapades push it to the limit. I hate to tell you how to live, but you're the person who signed the lease, and your wife is listed as an occupant. We don't have a problem with you, but your wife has to go."

"So you're telling me I have to leave?"

"No, sir. What I'm saying is either she leaves, or both of you go. It's completely up to you. You're welcome to stay, but Stacy is not. I'm sorry it's come to this."

Stacy didn't take it very well when I told her the choices I'd been given. She took it even worse when I told her I wasn't leaving. "So you're putting me out on the street?" she shrieked.

"Not really," I told her calmly. "You can go to Suzy's. If I leave with you, then *I'll* be on the street, because I have nowhere else to go—and you know damn well I'm not going to Suzy's, so I have no other choice. As usual, it was your actions that caused this to happen, Stacy, not mine. I really think you should consider anger management classes. I don't know what it is that has you so uptight all the time, but it's ruining us."

She didn't have anything to say to that, and moved out immediately.

I spent the next six months alone at the apartment, and enjoyed every minute of it. I worked overtime whenever I wanted, and paid most of the remaining past-due bills and hospital co-pay collection accounts that were killing my credit rating. I actually saw my score turn around and start heading back in the positive direction. I heard from Stacy occasionally, but she always wanted something; it was never to see how I was doing or to discuss our marriage, which was now in its ninth year. She usually wanted me to come by and bring her cigarettes or money to pick up prescriptions; she was still abusing the Xanax and pain pills.

I started visiting Cynthia, again for companionship only; we went out when it was convenient. We always had a good time, but the chemistry between us still didn't ignite the spark to rekindle a romance. She'd been seeing someone, but it didn't work out for her, so we basically provided mental therapy for each other.

Sometime after the first of the year in 2003, Stacy called to inform me that Shawn had gotten in trouble again, and had been sent to jail for a six-month sentence. I don't know why she made a point of telling me; I couldn't have cared less at that point.

Things seemed to be turning around for Cynthia and me. I began to develop serious feelings for her, and I felt she was reciprocating; yet I was legally married, and it was my opinion (although she never said it) that she'd decided to hold back on admitting her true feelings for fear of getting hurt.

I searched the Internet until I found a new 2002 Firebird still on a dealer's lot; they'd been discontinued in 2002, and finding a new one was not an easy task. The closest dealer was three hundred and fifty miles away. I contacted the dealership by phone and worked out a deal, then went to Credit Union. Because of the efforts I'd made to repair my credit situation, they agreed to loan me the money. My

Dad and I went on a road trip to trade in the Mustang. It was a very happy time in my life, but sadly, it would be short-lived.

Everything was going great for me. Because of my growing feelings for Cynthia, I was seriously contemplating filing for divorce. Stacy, however, ruined everything. She and her Mom had gone to the apartment manager where I lived and must have caught him in a good mood. Stacy told the manager she'd completed a course in anger management, and asked if he'd agree to let her come back to my apartment. She promised to behave and made her usual campaign promises; she had a knack for telling people what they wanted to hear.

I'd gone to see a doctor about having severe headaches and came home to find Stacy in the apartment.

After she took the time to explain how she'd gotten permission to return, she popped the hell out of my bubble. "I'd like for you to call and listen to the messages on the phone. I don't know your code," Stacy said icily.

I knew it wasn't going to be good news; the tone of Stacy's voice assured me of that fact. I called and listened to the message. *Jonny, this is Cynthia. What's going on? I called, and a woman claiming to be your wife answered the phone. I think you owe me an explanation, so call me. I want to know what's going on!*

"And I think you owe me an explanation, too!" Stacy shouted.

What was I supposed to do? I was married to her, and certainly didn't need a lot of legal trouble with lawyers. Even though Cynthia and I hadn't slept together, it wouldn't look good in court, so I had to break things off with Cynthia. Looking back now, I realize I should have left the apartment and moved to my parents' house. I could have arranged with the manager to pay for the apartment and utilities until the lease ended, and simply left Stacy there. Then I could have filed for divorce and kept my budding relationship with Cynthia going—but as they say, hindsight is always 20/20.

I was duped again by my own stupidity.

16

Put it in Shawn's Room!

Upon Stacy's return, I learned Suzy had been hit with an eviction notice for noise complaints; at least, that was the reason stated on the eviction notice. Shawn's constant trouble with the law, prompting frequent police visits, couldn't have set well with the neighbors, who I'm sure played a decisive role in the decision. The eviction notice must have scared the hell out of Stacy's Mom; she certainly didn't want the tribe of vigilantes at her house. I'm sure beyond a reasonable doubt that this event alone is what prompted the visit to the manager's office. Stacy needed somewhere to live, and her Mom made it a priority to get her back into my apartment. Lucky me.

Suzy had moved in with her current boyfriend at that time, but it didn't take long for the guy to realize what he'd gotten himself into. Shawn's room and board was being taken care of by the state's most gracious and accommodating penal system.

Stacy managed to keep up the ruse of being the good, kind, and gentle wife for about six weeks; then all hell broke loose again. Suzy's relationship with the boyfriend was floundering, and her never-ending phone calls to Stacy caused quite a stir. Stacy was beginning to show signs of mental distress; it seems her little angel was upset, which caused Stacy to get upset. And as they say, if Momma ain't happy, ain't nobody happy.

The destruction started again. Stacy and I had just reached a milestone: ten long, hard years of marriage. But the clock had started its countdown; time was running out for us as a married couple. The building blocks of our marriage were crumbling at the foundation, but I wasn't consciously aware of it yet.

It was over an hour's drive to take Stacy to see Shawn in jail. Poor Stacy couldn't understand why the legal system had targeted her son; she never did grasp the concept that it was Shawn's fault. I did, however, and I reveled in it. I didn't have a problem telling him he'd been the one in the wrong, and that contrary to his beliefs; he was not above the law.

On my first visit, Stacy and Shawn talked on the telephone, looking at each other through the clear plastic glass, for about fifteen minutes before he asked to speak to me. I looked at him for a long moment and asked, "So, what do you think about that badge now, boy? You still say that badge don't mean shit?"

"Okay, I don't need to hear your smartass comments," he snarled.

"Too bad, but don't you wish you'd have heard them before, when I kept telling you it was all going to catch up with you?"

"Okay, you've made your point. Just put Mom back on the phone."

The score was Jonathan one, Shawn zero. I really felt like this was a game, and I'd won this one.

Of course, I had to listen to the wrath of Stacy all the way back home that evening, but I'd been stewing on it the whole drive up, just waiting for the opportunity to say what I did. It was the highlight of my existence that day, and it was well worth it. I'd learned how to tune her out anyway, which made her even more angry.

Stacy was reverting back to her old self, and it didn't take very long for her to get there. She seemed to remember her hatred of bedroom doors; unlike one of our previous residences, in which she'd kicked a hole in all three, this time her choices were limited to the one. She didn't waste any time putting a hole in it—and it was my fault, she said.

One day I opened the phone bill, and was shocked to find that I owed over $1,200. Shawn had been calling collect from jail. He knew my work schedule, and always waited until I'd left before he'd call. He'd been calling in excess of *twenty times* a day. When I cornered the lioness in her den, I shook the bill at her and said,

"This won't happen again, Stacy. I'll take care of this problem right now."

"What are you going to do, asshole, cut the phone off like you did last time?"

"No, I need the phone for work; they can't call me for overtime if I cut it off."

It was an easy enough fix. I called the jail, and had them block their phone system from calling my number. Problem solved, on my end anyway. It made life more difficult to be around Stacy, to say the least—but Shawn was street-smart. Stacy had taught him well. He found a way around my plan, but it didn't hurt me, as I'd find out soon enough from Stacy's Mom.

I answered the phone one evening the next month to hear her ranting about her phone bill. Shawn had been calling her house, and she'd three-way the call to my apartment. That only worked for one month, until she followed my example and had her number blocked. He then tried it with my parents, but he should have known he wouldn't get away with *that*. "Would you tell the little asshole to quit calling my house collect?" my Dad told me irritably one day. "I'm not accepting his calls, and it's really getting aggravating."

I told him how to fix it, which he did. Then Shawn tried *another* way (he was a resourceful lad, I'll give him that). He'd get some of his fellow inmates to call their friends and relatives, then three-way the calls to our apartment. Again, this only lasted thirty or so days until I'd receive calls from very angry people, mostly relatives of inmates. It usually went like this: "Hello, this is so and so and I just got my phone bill. The calls for your son amount to over $300!" cried the angry woman on the phone.

"My bill was over $1,200," I replied laconically. "I'll trade ya." She didn't appreciate my attempt at humor at all; in fact, I upset her terribly. She wanted to know what I was going to do about it. "I'm not going to do anything about it," I told her flat-out. "I have my own bill I'm still paying on."

"Do you expect me to pay for your son's phone calls?" the irate woman demanded.

"Did I tell you to transfer the calls to my phone, or did you do it on the presumption that I was going to reimburse you?" I asked calmly.

"Shawn told me you'd reimburse me, so yes, I *do* expect you to make good."

"Forget it. First of all, he's not my son. I'm just married to his mother, I'm sorry to say. Second, you should have asked me on the first call if I'd be willing to pay."

"Well, I *did* ask your wife, and she said it was okay!"

"She doesn't have a job, ma'am, but you're more than welcome to take it up with her. I'm not paying the bill, sorry."

A couple days later, the woman's husband called and tried to threaten me. "I'm gonna have to take you to court if you don't reimburse me!" he declared.

"Okay, that's fine," I told him. "You do what you have to do."

I called his bluff; he knew he didn't legally have a leg to stand on, but obviously thought I didn't know that. I'm sure he contacted an attorney and was told that the judge would hold him responsible for accepting the calls, and without some form of verbal agreement from me, he couldn't expect to receive repayment. It was Stacy they'd have to subpoena to court; she'd been the one to say she'd repay, not me, and I'd already told them she didn't have a job. His only option was to try the bluff. I never heard from him again, and the phone calls from Shawn stopped—except for the occasional sympathetic person who'd allow him one phone call every couple of days.

I came out on the big end of the stick. It eventually cost me $100 to repair the door Stacy kicked the hole in; well, it was actually $50 for each time she kicked the hole in the door, because she did it twice, but that was a hell of a lot better than receiving more $1,200 phone bills.

Her newest form of punishment was slamming the front door. Now, if she'd have taken time to think about her actions, she'd have remembered that this had gotten her in trouble the last time, and caused her to be asked to leave. But Stacy's actions were always about two days ahead of her clear-thinking process, due to the amount of pills she was abusing. I knew the complaints were going to start again, so I gave my notice to vacate at the end of my lease. I didn't want another warrant of eviction to be placed on my front door. I had a good relationship with the manager, and wanted to keep the option open in case I ever needed to rent from him again.

I felt at this point that my actions put me in quite a dilemma, which I knew I had to deal with. On my next visit to Dr. Kashadi, I related the events up to the notice to vacate, and hoped his advice would ease the conflict my conscious mind was currently battling over; should I keep moving forward, or count my losses and get out? Deep down, I knew he'd tell me to get out, but he couldn't legally make the decision. He could only give me advice on the path I chose to tread.

"I know you pretty well by now, Jonathan," he told me after I laid out my dilemma. "I know you are not a quitter."

"Yes, but this time it's not an issue of heart versus head. It's more head versus head."

"Please explain what you are trying to say," he said, intrigued.

"I don't think my heart matters anymore. I don't have many feelings left for Stacy, but my head is being pulled in two different directions. You're right—I'm not a quitter, and that part of me's saying I should give it one last try; to go for broke, so to speak. The other is saying I must be a glutton for punishment. How long am I going to allow Stacy to drag me down and trample all over me until I cry 'Uncle' and give up?"

He shook his head. "You are fighting a battle that has no winning solution, Jonathan. Either way, you lose in some respect. If you give it one last try, you are allowing yourself to be trampled on; if you choose the other option and leave, knowing you like I do, you will spend the rest of your life pondering the 'what if' issues'. So you have to ask yourself, which is the lesser of the two evils for you? Dealing with the 'what ifs,' or giving it one last conscious effort to make it work?"

After a moment's thought, I replied, "I believe if I go into one last try with the attitude that it's either going to make or break me, I'll have inner peace with myself. At least I'll get some type of solace in knowing I gave it my all. That seems to be the way I'm leaning."

"Then it appears you have your answer," he said. "At least this time, you would be going into it with your eyes wide open, instead of having delusions that a miracle is going to occur."

*   *   *

The people who knew me best, my family and a few select co-workers, understood my decision and stood behind me. I heard the same advice from one of my better friends again: *"What doesn't kill you only makes you stronger!"* Other than *"The wheels may turn slowly, but they do turn,"* it was definitely one of the best pieces of advice I'd ever been given concerning Stacy. I'd become a stronger person, and I knew the end was near.

When it came time to move, I wanted a one bedroom apartment; but since Shawn was close to being released, I let Stacy's arguments sway me, and decided to take a two bedroom apartment instead. Maybe this time he'd listen to my advice, and see the errors of his ways.

We moved in the day Shawn was released from jail. One of my better co-worker friends helped me with the move. There wasn't that much to move, since Stacy had previously sold most of the stuff we'd had in storage. As my friend and I brought stuff in from the truck, I'd ask Stacy where she wanted it placed. Other than the obvious, our bedroom furniture, she seemed to have the same answer for everything: "Put it in Shawn's room!"

"Damn, Stacy, why don't we just make it a lot easier and put *everything* in his room?"

"I'm just excited he's finally coming home. Aren't you?"

"I could hardly sleep last night, Stacy," I said very sarcastically.

"You've really become a smartass!" she spat. "Suzy and I are going out after the truck is unloaded. We want to fix Shawn's room up for him so he'll be happy."

"Stacy, I think that after being in jail, sleeping in a cardboard box would be a pleasure."

Reluctantly, I gave Stacy the checkbook, since he was coming home that night. I'd decided to give her the benefit of the doubt, thinking that maybe her attitude and mood swings would improve when her baby came home. Who knew; it was worth a shot. I wasn't happy to find she'd spent over $200, but I'd made an effort to make Stacy happy, since our marriage was in the balance.

When we picked up Shawn from jail that evening, he related how he should have listened to me and his Mom, how he thought he knew everything and it took six months in jail to realize that we weren't as stupid as he thought—we really did know what we were talking about.

He managed to stay on his newfound righteous path for about two weeks before he went astray again.

I'd kept up my working overtime to alleviate some of the financial stress that had driven a wedge between Stacy and me. While we didn't see each other as much, having money to pay the bills on time did help our attitudes—until Suzy started having trouble with her boyfriend again. Shawn had met a girl and spent a lot of time with her away from home, which only opened the door for Suzy to spend more time at our apartment. As I mentioned earlier, Stacy and Suzy simply couldn't cohabitate together for very long. The riffs between them slowly escalated, and I saw the snowball swell as it rolled downhill. Of course Stacy was still scared of Suzy and wouldn't stand up to her, which left me to do the dirty work. I didn't have a problem with it; I'd tell her like it was. I wouldn't tolerate her *I'm better than you are* attitude in my house, and she knew it; I didn't have a problem having her forcefully removed from this apartment too if it were necessary.

Christmas, which was Stacy's favorite time of the year, was just around the corner, and she always took great pride in decorating her tree. I came home one afternoon after working the 8 to 4 shift and walked into the apartment to see the tree lying on its side. The apartment was deathly quiet, and our bedroom door was shut. I opened the door and saw Stacy in bed. I assumed she was asleep and started to close the door when she growled, "What the hell do you want?"

"What happened here today?"

"Just leave me the hell alone!"

"Okay," I said, and shut the door.

I went back into the family room, stood the tree back up, and was replacing the fallen ornaments when I heard a loud ruckus from the direction of the bedroom. Stacy had opened and slammed the bedroom door against the wall stop. She came marching down the hall, walked over to the tree, and turned it back over again.

"What did you do that for?" I asked.

"Leave me alone, you bastard! If I wanted the tree back up, don't you think I would have done it?"

"It seems to me if you wanted it up, you wouldn't have tipped it over twice. What the hell is going on, Stacy?"

"Suzy pissed me off."

"So why did you take it out on the Christmas tree?"

"I don't care about Christmas anymore! Between you and Suzy, you've ruined it for me."

"How did I ruin it?"

"I asked you to move me away from this area! I can't stand to be around Suzy, and if you'd have moved me away, I wouldn't have to be near her."

"Stacy, I think you're missing the point. You're the parent; she's the child. Take charge of her like you try to do with me. And it doesn't matter if we moved to Timbuktu; she'd follow you. You two can't live with each other, but you can't live without each other either. You're gonna have to cut the umbilical cord eventually."

"Oh, go to hell!" she screeched, and stormed back into the bedroom, slamming the door. I'm sure the sound resonated to the neighbors in the adjoining apartments. I still had no idea what had happened that day, and didn't until Suzy came in. To my request for information, the girl said sullenly, "Mom went off the deep end because she's out of Xanax, and I won't give her any of mine. The bitch is crazy."

I heard the bedroom door slamming up against the wall stop. Again.

"Let me tell you one thing, Suzy!" Stacy shouted. "I'm going into withdrawals and I need my medicine. As many Xanax as I've given you, and you're gonna let me go into withdrawals? I could die!"

"You're a psycho bitch!" Suzy shouted at her Mom.

"Okay, I think this has gone on long enough," I said. "Suzy, you should leave before this gets out of hand. Give her a couple of pills; she's given you a lot of hers. If both of you would take them as prescribed, this wouldn't be a problem."

"I'm not giving the crazy bitch anything," Suzy said, and stormed out of the apartment.

"Well, thanks one hell of a lot, asshole." Stacy said to me. "Now what am I supposed to do? I guess you'll have to take me to the emergency room!" she cried, as she walked into the bathroom.

"No, I'm not doing that anymore. Take your pills as prescribed, or I'll have your ass committed. I'm tired of this! You want to go to the ER, take yourself."

"You know, you're a real bastard. I hate your sorry ass!" She threw a can of something, hairspray or aerosol Lysol at me, I don't remember which it was, but it hit me on my right side towards the bottom of my rib cage. It didn't hurt all that bad, but two days later I went to see Dr. Syriana for my cortisone shot, and he saw the yellow-purple bruise when I took off my shirt.

"What happened to cause that bruise?" he asked suspiciously.

I had to think fast and said, "I reached over to cut off the alarm clock a couple days ago, and my rib cage hit the corner of the nightstand."

I could tell by the look on his face that he didn't believe me. "Let's take an X-ray of it just to be sure," he said dubiously.

"No. That's not necessary, Doc. It doesn't hurt too much."

"My friend, you could have a broken rib, and it could puncture your lung if you're not careful—so let's take an X-ray."

I knew there was no getting around it. I complied. He came back into the room later, and said I had two cracked ribs. "Are you sure you don't want to tell me what really happened?"

"I'm okay. If it gets any worse, I'll let you know."

"You want something for pain?"

"No, my wife would take all you give to me. I'm okay, Doc."

I know by law that doctors have to report when a child is suspected of being abused, but I'm not sure of the laws concerning adults. He did ask me to schedule a follow-up appointment in ten days. On that visit, he never discussed my shoulder at all; it was my ribs he was concerned about. He knew; his eyes said it all.

Stacy asked me on December 20th if I intended to give her money to buy Christmas gifts. "You said you weren't buying anything this year," I reminded her.

"I didn't mean it. I was just mad when I said that."

"I'll give it to you Tuesday when I get paid."

"That's not going to work, Jonathan; Tuesday is Christmas Eve. What the hell are you thinking?"

"I'm thinking you need to get a damn job, Stacy."

"Do you really think I could get a job and get paid before Tuesday?"

"No, but you could have gotten a job last month and gotten a paycheck by now."

"You expect me to believe that after all the overtime you've been working, you don't have any money to give me now?"

"Yes, that's exactly what I'm saying. Someone has to pay all the bills."

"I can't believe your sorry ass," she snarled. "You know I need to buy gifts, and you didn't set aside any money."

"The bills don't stop because it's Christmas."

"Nobody pays bills in December, don't you know that?"

"I'm not even going to respond to that comment. You'll get your money on Tuesday."

"How much are you giving me?"

"Five hundred dollars."

"How the hell do you expect me to buy for the kids and our parents with only $500?"

"Stacy, your kids are adults now. It's not like Santa Claus is coming and they expect a bunch of presents under the tree. Give Suzy, Shawn and my son $100 apiece, and that leaves $100 for my parents and the same for yours."

"That's not enough," she insisted.

"Ok, I'll give you $750."

I'd forgotten about her oldest son. He and his wife had recently had a baby, I had a soft spot for small children, and he was the only one of Stacy's offspring I actually liked.

"I need at least $1,000!" she said.

"You're not going to get it."

Or so I thought. Obviously, her scheming head had already formulated a plan. Later she declared, "I need to pick up three prescriptions. Can you at least give me a check for that, or do I have to take it out of the Christmas money?"

I'd taken her name off the checking account after the rent fiasco a couple of years back. "I'll give you a check, but it should be under $20," I told her. "Don't write it for any more than that."

"Jonny, insurance isn't going to pick up my Xanax prescription, because it's too soon to refill. I'm sure I'll have to pay full price, so the check will be a little bit more. It shouldn't be more than $50, though."

"Whatever!" I said, rolling my eyes. "And you know what? I don't want to hear the word *Xanax* anymore. You really need to get off that stuff before it kills you. Your body is probably toxic by now."

I was working the midnight shift the week of Christmas, and Stacy had arranged for all her kids, her parents and my son to be at our apartment. "You'll come home Christmas Eve morning and go to bed, right? You need to get up about five o'clock."

"I doubt it. There's going to be overtime, and I plan to work over onto the 8 to 4 shifts Christmas Eve and Christmas Day. I can't turn down triple time for sixteen hours both days, not as bad as we need money."

I lingered around work that Tuesday morning after shift change; I had to wait for the bank to open at nine before I went home. My paycheck had already gone in by direct deposit, but I needed to withdraw the cash for Stacy. I gave her the cash when she woke up that morning.

"Don't forget, you're supposed to give me a check for my prescriptions. Can you give it to me before you go to bed?"

"Yeah, I'll give it to you now."

I wasn't thinking—for some reason, I trusted her to do what she'd said and buy prescriptions. Before I left for work that night I asked how much the check was written for, as I needed to record it in my checkbook register.

"Can't you see I'm busy wrapping gifts? I'm not sure where the receipt is; can I look for it later?" Stacy said.

"Yeah, that'll be okay. I'm working over in the morning, don't forget."

I didn't find out the actual total until I was able to find out that the check had cleared the bank for the written total of $335. I wasn't all that surprised. It's a good thing I'd worked a lot of overtime to cover it, or it would have been returned for non-sufficient funds.

I came home the next afternoon, Christmas Eve, called my son to tell him to wake me up if he'd like to when he arrived, and then I went to bed. Stacy was mad that I didn't get up at seven to see her kids open their gifts; I actually couldn't have cared less. My son did come into the bedroom and talk to me for a few minutes. I worked over again on Christmas Day. I don't remember what I bought Stacy that year, but I gave it to her when I got home.

It came as no surprise that the only gift I had to open that Christmas Day was from my son. Stacy and her kids hadn't bought me one damn thing. I didn't expect anything from Stacy's oldest son; in fact he'd called me at work a couple of weeks before and asked if there was anything I needed in particular, but I told him not to worry about me, I'd rather he use the money for his new daughter. I'd already arranged to see my parents when the night shift was over that Friday.

Stacy and I did go out that New Year's Eve, but I can't remember where we went or what we did. It must not have been remarkable.

It was during the month of February that I started sleeping on the couch.

Financially, the first quarter of 2004 was very good for me; I worked over almost every day, beginning in mid-February and throughout the month of March. If I wasn't working the midnight shift, I'd get called in unless I was working 4 to 12, and then I volunteered to stay over. I worked twenty-three midnight shifts in a row, and forty-three consecutive days without a day off. Out of the forty-three days, I believe thirty-four were sixteen hours days.

Sometime in late spring of that year, Shawn started with his tricks again. He and his girlfriend had gotten an apartment together. Suzy and her boyfriend had broken up, and of course she took Shawn's bedroom. I was getting ready for work one afternoon when the phone rang. The woman introduced herself as a neighbor of Shawn's in their apartment complex. She wanted to know if I had the car at my apartment yet.

"What car?" I asked, baffled.

"Shawn said he and you were going out of state yesterday to pick up the car I bought from him," she said pleasantly.

"Umm . . . I'm sorry, ma'am, but I don't know what you're talking about."

"Oh, maybe he hasn't gotten around to asking you yet," she said brightly. "How do you like that Mustang?"

"Well, ma'am, I don't have it anymore. I bought a Firebird, and I didn't really care for the Mustang."

"It probably brought a lot of money, didn't it?"

"Not really," I replied, confused as hell. "I guess I got a decent amount for a trade-in, but I wouldn't say I got a lot of money."

"I can't imagine a 1967 Mustang Shelby 2+2 not bringing a good amount of money," she said dubiously.

Uh-oh. "Ma'am, my Mustang was a 2001. I didn't have a Shelby."

"Oh." She was quiet for a moment, the said, "You're sure you don't mind selling the Impala? My husband is going to be *so* surprised when he comes home. He's serving in the Middle East right now, and wants that car really bad. I certainly appreciate you letting it go."

"What Impala?"

"Excuse me?"

"Ma'am, I have no idea what you're talking about!"

A note of worry had finally crept into her voice. "Well, Shawn said you were willing to sell the 1964 Impala you own. I gave Shawn $800 for the car, and you were supposed to be going out of state to pick it up yesterday."

"I'm sorry to tell you this, ma'am," I said slowly, "but you've been conned. I don't own anything but a 2002 Firebird."

After a long and ominous silence, she said, "Well, then, if you see Shawn, have him call me, please. He has some explaining to do. I work in a lawyer's office, and had my boss draw up an eight-page contract, which Shawn signed."

Stacy came in before I left, and I relayed the conversation to her. However, she didn't get upset with Shawn; she was mad at me for telling the woman the truth. "Why didn't you go along with the story until I can talk to Shawn and find out what he's done?" she demanded. "Don't you ever think?"

"I just told you what he's done, and no, I'm not playing along with any of his lies," I said impatiently. "It looks to me like he's gonna be going back to jail! I guess he hasn't learned his lesson yet."

Shawn called me at work, and he also tried to give me hell for telling the truth—but I had no patience with his stupidity, so I hung up on him. When I got home late that night, Stacy was sitting at the kitchen table waiting for me with vengeance in her eyes. "I just want you to know that Shawn could be arrested if the woman files charges," she said in a dangerous voice.

"Well, he should be. I'm going to bed."

"You need to take me to the ER, I'm out of Xanax. This whole ordeal has me so upset I don't know how many I've taken today. Thanks to you, this has *not* been a good day."

I snorted. "I'm not going to the ER. If you need to go, then you go. And this isn't my fault. Keep on taking up for him, Stacy, blame me if you want, but I'm not going to lose any sleep over it."

"Well, Shawn is on the way over to talk to you. He's very upset."

"Stacy, I don't give a damn what he is! I'm going to sleep."

I'd probably been asleep about thirty minutes when Stacy woke me up to say Shawn wanted to talk to me. "Get up!" she demanded.

"Leave me alone. I'm not getting up."

I went back to sleep, but was eerily aware of someone's presence standing over and watching me. I felt something wet on my back and opened my eyes; Stacy was standing over me with a pitcher of water. "Get up or I'll pour the rest of this on you!" she declared.

"You do it, and I'll call the police." She left me alone after that.

I continued working all the overtime I could get. I especially liked to be called in, or work over, onto the midnight shift so I could keep from being at home at night.

Stacy and I rarely talked anymore. If we did, it was usually an argument. I'd give her enough money every week to buy food and necessities, but I kept my checkbook at my Mom's for fear Stacy or Shawn would forge my signature. She'd recently started going through my wallet while I slept, which caused me to start hiding paper money in my car—again. I'd open the small access door to the fuse panel and put folded bills inside.

As she'd warned, the woman Shawn had scammed filed papers with the court for fraudulent activities. When the court date neared, Stacy called the courts and had the case continued, stating Shawn was in the process of seeking legal representation and would be away at boot camp. In actuality, Shawn thought the whole ordeal was funny, and felt confident he'd get away with it.

Living conditions around the household continued to deteriorate. One day in April, I found Stacy anxiously waiting for me at the door when I came home one afternoon. "What's this, Jonathan?" she demanded, holding up a very short straw.

"How many guesses do I get?" I asked.

"I'm serious, Jonathan! What's this?"

"It looks like a piece of a straw. Where did it come from?"

"I found it in the dryer. I washed a load of clothes today. Do you have anything to say?"

"Yes, as a matter of fact I do. Did you happen to wash my blue jeans?"

She didn't appreciate my attempt at humor. "I want you to take a drug test, *now!*" she said adamantly.

"Okay, where is it?"

"You'll have to go to the drugstore and buy one."

"I'm not buying it. I'm not doing drugs. It must be Shawn's."

"He said it was yours. It's funny, he said you'd say it was his. So are you going to take the drug test or not?"

"Stacy, I told you I'd take it, but I'm not paying for it."

"How convenient!" she said, with a smirk on her face. "That's okay, I'll get the test, and if it's positive, I'll take you for everything you have."

"Stacy, you've already done that. You sold most of it, remember?"

She called her Mom on the phone and explained the situation. Her Mom told her to come over and she'd give her the money. I'm sure the dollar signs were flashing in her Mom's eyes. Stacy came back with the test, and handed me a plastic cup to pee in. I walked towards the bathroom.

"Hold on! You're not going in there by yourself."

"Why not? I know how to use the big boy potty."

"I'm going to watch, just to make sure you actually pee in the cup."

"Okay, you can hold it if you want to," I said casually.

"You might ever be so lucky!" she responded.

It took a while with her staring at me, but I finally provided her sample.

She immediately went to work reading the instructions and performing the test. It came back negative. You'd think she'd be happy I wasn't doing drugs, but she was disappointed. She went downstairs and got a woman neighbor friend of hers to come up and assist. She insisted I pee again.

After she had the second sample she and the neighbor went about the procedure—and lo and behold, it was negative too! The neighbor woman was happy, and couldn't understand why Stacy wasn't. "Damn, Stacy, you act like you're pissed off, you should be glad it's negative," the neighbor said.

"I guess you'd better test Shawn," I told her.

She threw the cup at me. Some of it got on my pant legs; the rest went on the kitchen cabinet doors and the floor.

I'm not sure if the straw in the dryer was an isolated incident, or if it had been an issue before and I wasn't made privy to it. As I've said earlier, Stacy's actions superseded her rational thinking processes—and by the time she realized what she'd done, it was too late.

I was sitting at the computer one afternoon when there was a knock at the door. Stacy answered, and a Sheriff's Deputy asked for me. He handed me a letter and left.

"Oh, I forgot to tell you about that!" Stacy said anxiously, when she saw who'd sent the letter. "Don't even read it, Jonny, give it to me and I'll tear it up."

It seems Stacy had contacted an attorney and wanted to file for divorce. As I read the letter, Stacy tried to make jokes and laugh it off, but the more I read, the angrier I got. The letter stated Stacy intended to vacate the apartment, in which she currently resided, on or before May 31, 2004. The reason being, she was in fear of both her and her children's lives, due to my non-stop use of illegal substances. It stated that she had tried many times, all in vain, to convince me to stop said use of these substances, and had repeatedly urged me to seek professional help for my drug addiction, yet I'd refused. Therefore, due to the circumstances, Stacy was to find adequate housing for her and her children and I, the defendant, was to pay the cost of the monthly rent or mortgage and all the necessary utilities to ensure Stacy was able to live in the lifestyle to which she was accustomed. It went even further; I was to pay all her living expenses, provide her medical insurance, and give her the sum of $200 a week for the remainder of her natural life.

"Isn't that funny?" Stacy asked when I finished reading it.

"Oh, it's just hilarious, Stacy. Your lawyer is one hell of a comical guy!"

"Jonny, I called and told him not to send it, I said I'd changed my mind, but he told me it had already been sent and to prepare you for when it arrived . . . but I forgot. I'm so glad I was here when it did come!"

"You told him I had a *drug addiction?*"

"Well, when I found that straw, I freaked out. I'm so sorry! Give me the letter and I'll dispose of it."

"No, I think I'll keep it. So you found the straw, automatically assumed it was mine, and did all of this without even talking to me about it?"

"I did ask Shawn, and he said it wasn't his, it was yours!"

"And you believed Shawn? The same Shawn who's been scamming people out of money and claiming he's getting a $17,000 bonus for joining the Army? Is that the Shawn you're referring to?"

"I said I was sorry, Jonny, what else can I say?"

"If anyone has a drug addiction, it's you. The tests I did were negative, both of them."

"I know, that's why I got so upset when you came up negative, I'd already called the lawyer. I'm so sorry for not believing in you."

"You're the one who needs professional help, Stacy."

"Can I have the letter?"

"No, I'm keeping it."

"What are you going to do with it?"

"I don't know yet. But I'm keeping it. It may come in handy in the future."

I had to hide the letter that day, but the next day I took it to work and kept it in my locker. She couldn't get to it there.

Stacy knew she'd messed up this time. She tried to rectify the situation, but it was no use—the damage had been done.

In June, Shawn came up with another of his ingenious ideas. He'd found a four wheel drive pickup in a person's yard with a sign on the windshield saying 'For Sale by Owner.' The guy wanted $4,000, and after talking with the con artist, he agreed that Shawn could make monthly payments. Well, Shawn hadn't even made the first payment when he saw a red sports car he wanted in someone's front yard. They wanted $10,000 for it. By his way of thinking, the pickup was worth $4,000, so he made a deal with the owner of the sports car. He gave her the truck, and promised to pay the remaining $6,000 when he got his sign-on bonus for joining the Army. This time, however, Stacy went down there with him, and signed an agreement with the owner of the sports car. Shawn immediately went to work on the car. He attached a fire extinguisher inside to make it resemble a nitrous oxide bottle, took out the passenger seat to lessen the weight, and then took it to the local drag strip, where he proceeded to strip out the clutch and transmission.

When the owner called to inquire about the first payment, which was late, Stacy told the owner not to worry. She'd make it right as soon as his bonus came. Stacy actually believed he was going into the Army and getting a sign-on bonus—and I thought *I* was naïve!

Our eleventh and final anniversary passed that year; needless to say, we didn't celebrate the occasion. What was the point? In any case, Stacy had begun thinking I was having an affair again. She demanded I show her my paycheck stubs to prove all the overtime I'd been working. She began scrutinizing the clothing I wore to work.

"You're wearing that to work?" she said one afternoon. I was working the 4 to 12 shift.

"Yes, why?"

"Do you think I'm stupid? Do you really expect me to believe you've been working overtime all those nights?"

"My check stubs prove it!" I snapped.

"Well, your boss will lie for you. I'm not stupid."

I disagreed, but I just said, "Stacy, I don't have time for this. I have to go."

I always kept a plastic cup from Hardee's or 7-11 and would fill it with iced tea before I left each day. "Here," Stacy said, "Don't forget your tea!" and proceeded to throw the entire cup on me, soaking my clothes. I had to change my shirt and pants, which was her sole purpose for throwing the tea onto me in the first place; she needed to delay me leaving the apartment so I couldn't meet up with my so-called girlfriend before work.

I was completely surprised when Stacy bought me a birthday present in July. She'd spent over $100 on Shawn's welcome-home-from-jail party and lots of money for Christmas, yet she hadn't spent one red cent on me. I don't know what prompted Stacy to buy me a birthday present that year. She gave me a shirt and I actually loved it. I decided I'd wear it to work that afternoon, but Stacy didn't like the idea at all once I put it on.

"That shirt looks very good on you!" she said, "You're not wearing that to work."

"Why not?" I asked.

"I bought you the shirt to wear when you and I go somewhere. I didn't buy it so you can look good for your girlfriend, so take it off."

"Oh come on, Stacy, stop being so ridiculous."

"I'm serious, Jonathan, take it off."

Just to shut her up, I did what she wanted and took it off. I went back to the bedroom to get another and came back. She was sitting on the couch with a pair of scissors cutting the shirt she'd just given me into lots of small pieces.

"What the hell did you do that for?" I asked.

"It looks too good on you, that's why!"

My days there were numbered.

*   *   *

The owner of the red sports car got a not-so-pleasant surprise when she received a visitor at her front door; the owner of the pickup truck. He said he'd seen it in her driveway too many times, and inquired as to why it was there. Once he was told the story of how it came to be at her house, they decided to check into Shawn a little further. Apparently they visited the courthouse and found that he was also on the court dockets for conning the first woman out of $800.

Somehow they managed to get in touch with her, and all three went to the prosecuting attorney with their stories. I was working the 4 to 12 shift, and for once actually turned down the overtime for the midnight shift. I was literally a basket case by this point. The thread holding my sanity in place was quickly unraveling. No one else wanted to work either, it turned out, and since I was the lowest in seniority, I was required to stay over. The next morning, I probably hadn't been asleep on the couch five minutes when there was a knock on the door.

Shawn had stayed over in his old room that night, and came out to answer the door. I don't remember where Suzy was; she may have been back with her boyfriend at that time. I honestly don't recall.

Shawn opened the front door to face three policemen. It's never a good thing when the police call you by name. "Hello, Shawn!" one officer said cheerfully. "I have a warrant here for your arrest."

"For what?" he asked.

"I'm not exactly sure. It's from another jurisdiction. I was told to pick you up, and they'll meet me at the city line. They can explain why."

The officer looked at me on the couch and asked if Mrs. David was here. "Yes, she's asleep," I said fuzzily.

"Which bedroom is she in, sir?" the officer asked.

"The end of the hall. I'll get her for you," I offered, and started to get off the couch.

"Stay right where you are. Do not leave the couch! Do you understand?"

What the hell? "Yessir."

"Mrs. David!" the officer said as he slowly walked down the hallway, hugging the wall. "This is the police. I want you to slowly open this door."

"Hold on! What's wrong? Why are the police here?"

"She doesn't have any weapons in there," I told the officer. "I don't own any guns." He didn't listen to me, and I guess I can't say I blamed him; I could have been lying, for all he knew.

"Mrs. David, I want you to crack open the door and let me see both of your hands, do you understand?"

"Yes, I'm coming," Stacy said meekly. The door opened just a crack, and both of Stacy's hands were visible.

"Okay, step back, ma'am," the officer said.

The officer opened the door and informed Stacy that she, too, was under arrest. He inspected the half-bath in the bedroom for weapons, and then told her she could put her clothes on in there. He handcuffed her once she was dressed, and both she and Shawn were hauled away.

I'd be lying if I said I was happy about what had just occurred. I'd tried to tell Stacy not to sign that agreement with Shawn, but as usual she wouldn't listen. I actually felt sad to see her cuffed and taken away. I know she hadn't felt sorry in the least when she'd had me arrested for stalking, or cuffed that day at her apartment and put into the mental institution—but then, I wasn't a firm believer in 'an eye for an eye.' Two wrongs don't make a right, but really, Stacy had it coming. I'd known it was only a matter of time before Shawn took her down with him.

I'd had no sleep and had to be back at work that afternoon at four, but first I had to drive to the police station in the next jurisdiction, where all three of Shawn's victims lived, to see what would be done with them. After three or four hours of waiting, Stacy was released on her own recognizance, but Shawn was held on $1,000 bond. I refused to pay the $100 to get him out on bail, so I had to listen to the wrath of Stacy all the way home. I had only one hour to sleep before it was time to go back to work, and Stacy made sure I didn't get that. She went about the house throwing and breaking things and calling me a multitude of four-letter words for not bailing her little angel out of jail. I finally decided it would be in my best interests to get up, take a shower, and go into work early to get away from her. Of course, I was hit by another can of something while dressing in the bathroom; then, after donning a pitcher of iced tea, I had to shower and change again.

"You throw one more thing at me and I'll personally call the police and have you arrested again!" I told her. "Do you understand what I'm saying, Stacy?"

"All I can say is, you're a worthless bastard for leaving your stepson in jail. You could give me the money to bail him out."

"That's right, Stacy, all of this is *my* fault. Turn it around on me. You know what? I've had it. My sister told me once that when I got a gut-full, I'd know it. Guess what, kiddo? My gut's full."

I walked out the door and called my lawyer, Mrs. Ingram, the minute I got to work, and made an appointment for the next morning. As luck would have it, I had to work over that night too. I went from Tuesday morning to late Thursday afternoon with no sleep at all. I couldn't come home that Thursday morning and go to sleep on the couch, since I had an appointment with Mrs. Ingram at 1:00 that afternoon. I'd be awake fifty hours before I had an opportunity to even start considering sleep.

17

I'll Represent You on
One Condition . . .

It was with much trepidation that I thought about my upcoming appointment with Mrs. Ingram; she always said exactly what was on her mind. I knew a lecture was in order, and I deserved it for going back to Stacy after the stalking incident. However, Mrs. Ingram was one hell of an attorney, and treated her clients as friends. She didn't see dollar signs when clients came in the door: she saw friends and acquaintances. Because of these redeeming qualities, she was my only choice to handle my divorce. Of course, I knew there was always the chance she might say she wouldn't represent me at all, considering my previous mistakes.

Mrs. Ingram had always thought well of my parents for tolerating and standing behind me through the years of torture we'd all experienced, so I figured it certainly wouldn't hurt to take one or both of them along to the appointment. I asked my Dad, and he agreed. Another reason I wanted someone to accompany me was because I was both physically and mentally exhausted, and I didn't want to forget any relevant facts that Mrs. Ingram might need.

Once we were called back to her office and the usual pleasantries were exchanged, we took our seats, and got down to the business at hand. "So what brings you to see me, Jonathan?" she asked solicitously.

"Divorce. I think it's time."

"It was time years ago," she replied darkly. "Tell me what's happened."

My Dad relayed most of the events of the past couple of years, and I sat there staring off into space—which really seemed to bother her. "Jonathan, are you sure this is what you want?" she finally asked. "If we start this procedure, are you going to change your mind midstream?"

"No, I'm just very tired." I explained about my lack of sleep.

"Are you still living with Stacy?"

"Yes, but I've slept on the couch since late February, and it's August now—so that makes six months."

She looked at me for a long moment before she asked, "So what are you going to do?"

"I want to leave and go back to their house." I said, indicating my Dad.

"Then go."

"I just can't walk away! Stacy will get me for abandonment."

She snorted. "No, she won't. She can't do that. You'll be leaving her with a roof over her head. When you're gone, she'll basically have everything she has now, except for you, and it sounds like she won't miss you anyway. It would be different if you blindfolded her, drove a hundred miles away, and left her on the side of a dirt road. That's more what you'd call abandonment, and you'd probably be arrested for that. So—when do you plan to leave?"

"Soon. Very soon."

"Okay, I have a few questions." She tapped her pencil on her desk a few times before she threw the first one at me. "Are you serious this time?"

"Yes, it has to be done."

"I'm glad you finally see that. Are you seeing anyone for help? Professionally, I mean."

"I'm seeing a psychiatrist."

"Have you seen a therapist?"

I shrugged. "I've seen one, but I haven't been in a while."

"I'll represent you on one condition, Jonathan," Mrs. Ingram said, looking at me closely. "I want you to see a therapist to help you get through this. I mean it—that's the only way I'll work with you.

If you don't show up for the first appointment, then don't come through my door again. I *will* call and find out if you went."

I held up both hands in mock surrender. "Yes, ma'am. I'll call and make an appointment when I get home."

"Oh no, I'm making the appointment for you right now." She picked up the phone and dialed a number; she knew it off the top of her head. She looked at me gravely as she waited, and when someone answered she said briskly, "This is Laura Ingram. May I speak to Gray Logan please? Thanks." After a short delay, she said, "Gray, this is Laura. I have a prospective client here, and he needs to talk to someone. When can you see him? Okay, he'll be there—I guarantee it."

She put the handset in its cradle and said to me, "Your appointment is next Tuesday. Here's his name, the time and the address. Remember: if you don't show, no deal, okay?"

"I'll make it to the appointment," I grumbled. "I promise."

I was as good as my word. I went to the appointment with Mr. Logan, and actually found it beneficial. I really liked him. He was easy to talk to, and made me feel very comfortable. "You have to call Mrs. Ingram and let her know I came to the appointment," I said as I settled in.

"I'll call her once we're done."

"Um, would you please call her now and let her know I'm sitting here in your office?"

He got up quietly and did as I wanted. I saw him every week after that, and looked forward to the appointments.

I don't remember what Stacy and I argued about a couple of days later, but I didn't have to pack my stuff; Stacy did it for me this time. She had all my belongings boxed and sitting by the front door. I made no effort to get off the couch, so she took all the boxes out to the parking lot and sat them on the hood and rear spoiler of my car.

Shawn came in an hour later, asking why there were boxes all over the car. Stacy explained the situation to him. "You better do something before someone steals it," he said.

I went out and put the boxes inside the car, set the alarm for thirty minutes earlier than normal, and went to sleep on the couch. The next morning I drove to my parents' house, unloaded all the boxes onto their back deck, and then went to work. I never returned to the apartment.

My lease was up in November. I called the office to notify them I'd vacated the premises; however, I informed them, Stacy was still living there. I promised to make the monthly rent payments until the end of the lease, and I gave them verbal notice I wouldn't be renewing. If they allowed Stacy to stay after November, I made it clear it would be entirely at their discretion; however, she'd be staying under a new lease without my name on it.

"Mr. David," the Manager said, "We require a written notice at least sixty days prior to lease termination."

"You'll have it tomorrow," I told him.

I called Mrs. Ingram to let her know I'd left the apartment and I needed to begin work on a separation agreement. With her permission, I was allowed to write my own legal separation agreement to save money. I modeled it after the agreement drawn up in my first marriage.

I wasn't a famous celebrity; my leaving Stacy didn't make headlines. People wouldn't be in line at their neighborhood supermarket, seeing 'Jonathan Leaves Stacy, Citing Abuse!' on the front pages of the *National Enquirer* or *Star* tabloids. I kept it relatively simple in the papers, and claimed 'Irreconcilable Differences' as the reason for our separation. I didn't see the need to make it any harder than necessary; Stacy would never sign the agreement if the papers portrayed her as the villain. In fact, I did everything possible to make the papers more attractive to Stacy. Even though I left in August of 2004, I agreed to pay the rent and all the utilities until the end of November. At the beginning of December, I offered Stacy $150 a week for living expenses.

Since we had no children together, the divorce could be finalized after six months of separation, provided we agreed on the terms. I could have stopped any form of financial assistance at the end of February, the end of the six-month period, but I agreed to pay her the weekly payment until the end of July 2005, one full year from the time I left. I would also continue to pay the cost to keep her medical insurance in effect, at least until the end of the month the divorce decree was signed and finalized by a judge.

I felt I was being more than fair in my offer, considering the circumstances. Did I have an ulterior motive? Of course I did. I made them attractive to get her signature. I'd relinquished the fight by leaving, which was entirely against my never-quit principles. However, I knew it was a no-win situation when I'd gone to my psychiatrist that day and asked for permission to give it one more shot. I had to accept it; I'd given it my all and, basically, I was tired of fighting. Did I expect the papers to be signed immediately? No, I was no longer that naïve; I knew Stacy well enough to expect some form of resistance. She'd use her 'give me an inch and I want a mile' principle. But I'd already formulated a backup plan, and was ready to throw it out on the table if necessary.

When Stacy saw my proposal for the first time, as expected, she balked and went straight to the defense. "I need more than $150 a week. Where am I supposed to live after November? I need money each week, starting now! I need medical insurance for at least two years!" she declared.

"Stacy, the only reason I'm paying the rent and utilities is because they're all under my name. I've already contacted the office and given written notice that I don't intend to renew. I've contacted the power, telephone, and cable companies and made arrangements for the utilities to be cut off December first."

"Well, it seems if you can pay close to $1,000 a month until December, you can afford to give me more than $150 a week!"

"So I take it you aren't signing the papers?" I asked.

"What does this tell you?" she said, as she tore them in half. "I'll get a lawyer!"

She expected me to cower down, she expected me to stumble and stutter, but I knew better. Neither she nor her Mom had the money to engage me in a lengthy court battle. I turned and walked away, which she wasn't expecting; I was standing up to her.

I got back in touch with Cynthia in late October. I wasn't going to be surprised if she told me to take a hike after I'd duped her and let Stacy move back in. She said she'd met someone after that event, but it didn't work out for her. With some trepidation and reserve, she agreed to see me again. However, I felt I was walking into an icebox when I went to her home that day. I couldn't say I blamed her; I fully understood her actions. What guarantee did she have I wouldn't do it again?

"Are your separation papers signed?" she asked.

"No, I'm still arguing the terms, but I promise you, Cynthia, it *will* happen this time. I'm getting a divorce."

"Yeah, well, I've heard that before," she responded.

"I don't expect you to welcome me back with open arms," I told her. "I know I have to prove myself to you. All I can ask is that you give me the chance to do that."

"You're here, aren't you?"

"Yes. I guess I'll have to take it one day at a time."

"Okay, but don't expect much from me for quite a while. This is going to take time, a long time."

"So, is there any chance you and I could have a relationship beyond friendship?" I asked.

"Time will tell." Cynthia had the upper hand. I knew I was at her mercy, but it's where I wanted to be.

We continued seeing each other weekly on my off days, and I eventually began staying at her house some nights, sleeping in the same bed. However, when I say *sleeping*, that's literally what we did; sleep, nothing else. She wasn't going to let her guard down and get hurt again.

I'd had my own phone line installed at my parents home to keep my parents from being pestered by Stacy's late night calls and, of course, for my privacy when talking to Cynthia. At the beginning of November, Stacy called me; she'd come up with a rebuttal to my separation papers. "I talked to the Apartment Manager, and he'll allow me to stay for six more months," she announced.

"Good for you," I answered.

"I need you to make the rent payments for those six extra months. It'll give me time to get a job and get established. Will you do that?"

I considered it, and said, "I'll pay the rent, but that's all."

"What about the utilities?"

"You'll have to put them in your name starting December first."

"And just where am I supposed to get the money to do that?" she asked fretfully.

"You just said you were going to get a job. If you start now, you'll have the money."

"The $150 a week is barely going to keep me afloat. I can't pay for the utilities too!"

"Stacy, I think we have a misunderstanding here. The $150 a week amounts to $600 a month, and *that's* what I'll use to pay the rent. I'm not paying the rent *and* giving you the money too."

"That's not right, Jonathan. If I make enough to pay the rent and the utilities, how am I supposed to feed myself, Suzy, and Shawn on $600 a month and still have money to live day by day?"

"Stacy, I'm sorry, but Suzy and Shawn are both legal adults, so they're not my responsibility. I'm married to you, not your kids; I'm offering the money for your benefit, not theirs. They're old enough to tend to themselves. If you want to let them sponge off you, don't cry to me about it."

"You're a real asshole, you know that?" she spat as she hung up the phone.

By the end of November, Cynthia began warming up to me a little—but she was a very long way from hot. Our nights together had progressed to include some embracing and occasional snuggling, but that's all. In her eyes, I was still on trial and hadn't proven myself. I wasn't in a position to argue and considered myself lucky to be with her, so I could only bide my time.

I tried every possible angle within my power to convince her it was over between Stacy and me. Part of me thinks she did believe me, or she wanted to; maybe it was Stacy that she was leery of.

Cynthia knew from past experiences that Stacy had a way of getting me to react.

When December arrived, I knew I'd be hearing from Stacy soon, asking for the weekly payments. She didn't let me down. I don't remember how, but she was still in the apartment in December. "So, are you going to pay me the money each week, like you said?"

"What money?" I asked, playing stupid.

"You told me if I signed the papers you'd give me $150 a week until the end of July."

"Yes, I did say that."

"So are you going to pay it or not?"

"No, not now I'm not."

"But you said . . ."

"Stacy, you didn't sign the papers," I snapped, cutting her off in mid-sentence. "I don't have to give you *anything*. I tried to be nice and make this amicable, but you tore the papers up in my face."

"I'll make a deal with you," she said. "I'll sign them today if you pay me until next December."

It was time for my back-up plan to come into play. She'd done exactly what I'd anticipated. "Nope, I'll only pay through July, and the amount is now $125 a week. Every month you delay, it drops by $25."

"Go to hell!" she said and hung up again.

I knew I hadn't heard the last of her; Christmas was coming, and she'd need money. *She'll call back!* I told myself. I knew it just as sure as I knew my own name. It only took a couple of days before Stacy called back with a counteroffer.

"I'll sign the papers today, on one condition!" she said.

"And what's that?" I asked.

"Two things," she said. "You know Christmas is coming, you agree to give me $150 a week for the month of December, and then you can drop it to $125 a week from January until the end of July."

"That sounds reasonable," I replied, "What's the second thing?"

"You agree to keep my health insurance in effect until the end of July."

"Stacy, I'll keep your insurance in effect until the end of the month the divorce is issued. I've already checked with the Insurance Company and that's all they'll do. If the divorce is issued on April 1, for example, you'll be covered the entire month. If it's issued on the last day of the month, then it ends that day. Sorry, I can't change their rules."

"But you *can* pay the premiums to keep it in effect, Suzy told me so."

"Is Suzy your legal advisor now?" I asked sarcastically.

"Don't be a smartass, Jonathan. I can't afford an attorney, and you know it. She does know a lot about the law; you have to give her credit for that."

"And I know a lot about space exploration, but that doesn't make me a rocket scientist. Stacy, as I've said, I've tried to make this as easy as possible for both of us. We both knew it was imminent. I'm basing the divorce on irreconcilable differences; I left out all the abuse issues. I'm offering to help you get on your feet, which I don't have to do unless ordered to by the courts. I just want it done in the easiest and fastest way possible. If this goes to court, the abuse issues will come up, and you know there's a very good chance I'll walk out without having to pay you anything at all. Tell your legal genius that if she wants to face Mrs. Ingram in court, Mrs. Ingram will relish the thought!"

She hung up on me. My phone rang again within thirty minutes. I was expecting it to be Cynthia, but it wasn't.

"Jonathan, this is Suzy. I don't know what your problem is! All Mom wants is for you to pay her insurance until the end of July. You're willing to pay the weekly payment, but not the insurance; you know her health is bad!"

"Suzy, I've already been over this with your Mom. You're more than welcome to call Mrs. Ingram. Do you want the number?"

"No, I don't. When do you expect the divorce to be final?"

"The six months are up in February. My lawyer said to expect to wait two months for them to be signed. I'd say sometime in April."

"Mom called the insurance company, and you can put her on the program they call COBRA. It'll cost almost $400 a month. It's not going to kill you to pay it for May, June, and July."

"Have your Mom give me a call," I said. I purposely gave Suzy the impression she'd convinced me to cooperate.

It was less than three minutes before the phone rang again. "Jonathan, you told Suzy to have me call you?" she said, trying to act like she was unaware of Suzy's and my conversation. "What's up?"

"Aren't you going to work?"

"Yes, the first of the year!"

"I bet you start on the first Tuesday of January, right?"

"What?" she said confused.

"Forget it. I was just being a smartass. Aren't you going back into the nursing field?"

"Yes, why?"

"They provide you insurance, so why the big deal?"

"Because if I take the insurance, I make less money per hour, and I can't afford to live. That's why I want you to help me out for the three months. By then I should be okay."

"So you're refusing insurance to bring home more money?"

"Right!"

"Okay, Stacy, here's what I'll do. I'll pay for COBRA until the end of July, but the $125 a week stops when the divorce is final."

"But I need that money too!" she cried.

"Stacy, you're not getting both. It's either $125 a week or COBRA, your choice."

"Damn you; it's either your way or the highway, isn't it?"

"Yes, dear, for the first time in over eleven years, it is! We can go to court if you're willing to take your chances."

"Damn you!" she said before she hung up, again.

It wasn't too long before the phone rang again, but it was Cynthia this time. "So, have you heard from Stacy?" she asked.

Every time Cynthia called me, that was always the first thing she'd ask. That was the reason I came to believe she *did* care about me; it was Stacy she didn't trust. "As a matter of fact," I told her,

"I just got off the phone with her. She's arguing over the papers as usual."

"She'll never sign the papers—get used to it. She'll drag this out forever." I could tell by the tone of Cynthia's voice that she firmly believed what she was saying—which only reinforced my beliefs about her even more.

"She'll sign," I said, "just wait and see. I really believe it's going to happen before the week is over."

"I'll believe it when I see it."

"And if it does happen, will it make things better between us?" I asked with a note of hope in my voice.

"It certainly won't hurt!"

"I'll take that as a positive sign."

Early the next morning, the phone woke me from a deep sleep. I looked at the clock to see that it was seven in the morning; probably Cynthia, I thought. She always got up at five in the morning. I was working the 4-12 shift that week, and had stayed up late watching "Matlock" on TV. I had gotten so I really liked the show; I'd watched it religiously every night when I was out with my shoulder those seven months. I answered the phone groggily, only to hear the she-devil's voice: "Jonathan, it's Stacy. I need to talk to you!"

"Stacy, please call me back in a couple hours, it's too early."

"Okay, but it's important. I want to make a deal on the papers."

"Call me back at nine," I said, and went back to sleep.

Cynthia called within thirty minutes, so I decided I might as well get up. I called Stacy back at eight. "What is it this time?" I asked.

"I'll make a deal with you."

"And what's that?"

"You have three more paychecks this month, the 15th, 22nd, and 29th, right?"

"I guess so, why?"

"If you'll give me the payments for those three weeks now, $375, I'll sign the papers. That will give me money for Christmas and you won't have to pay again until January."

"You'll sign the papers if I do that? Promise?"

"Yes, I'll sign them."

"Okay, meet me at the bank at 9:30. I'll call Renée, the Notary, and let her know we're coming."

"See you there!" she said, and hung up.

I purposely didn't call Cynthia with the good news. She'd just have something negative to say, and she wasn't the only one who didn't trust Stacy. I figured the she-devil might still try to pull a fast one on me if I was so close to getting her signature. I decided to wait until they were signed and I'd taken them to Mrs. Ingram's office before I said anything to Cynthia.

I arrived at the bank before Stacy, and sat at Renée's desk talking. I'd known her for years. She'd been previously employed by my Credit Union, but had moved on to the local bank for a better position and (of course) more money. Stacy arrived about five minutes later, pen poised to get it all over with.

"Don't you want to read the papers before you sign them?" I asked. "You tore the others up."

Stacy went about reading the normal information concerning when and where we'd been married, our lack of children, the issues concerning the apartment and weekly payments, and the medical insurance. On the second page, she stopped. "What's this mean?" she asked, tapping the page.

I looked. "It says if you move in with another man or another man moves in with you before the end of July, the weekly payments stop."

"That's not fair!" she said.

"Why not?"

"It'll be none of your business what I do—the clause above this says we'll respect each others' privacy during the separation! So am I to assume you can live with another woman?"

"Yep!"

"But I can't live with another man!"

"It doesn't say you can't. It just says that if you do, then the weekly payments stop. Why should I support you if another man is taking on that responsibility?"

"Well, what if Suzy gets a job and brings home paychecks? Does it stop then too?"

"Nope, I'm not married to Suzy. We've been through this, Stacy. I'm helping to support you, but if another man wants to, then my obligation is finished."

"Then why is it okay for you to move in with a woman? Shouldn't it be both ways?"

"Are you paying me money each week, Stacy?"

"Hell, no."

"Okay, then. If you were paying me and I moved in with a woman, wouldn't you want to stop?"

"I'm not signing the papers with that in there," she said firmly. "You take that out and I'll sign."

"Okay," I said, and began collecting the copies. "Renée, thanks for your time. I'm sorry to have bothered you."

"So you're just going to leave, is that it?" Stacy cried.

"Yes, I'm tired of arguing with you. I'm not taking the clause out; I have every right for it to be there, since I'm paying you. Would you expect me to pay it if you remarried before July?"

"No, that's different!" she said.

"Not in my eyes it's not. We'll talk about this in January. Don't worry, once they're signed, I'll pay you what you're owed for December." I said goodbye to Renée, and turned to walk away. I'd gotten about four steps towards the door when Stacy spoke. I knew she would; I'd called her bluff again. My comment about not talking again until January did it; she realized she wouldn't get any money for Christmas.

"Okay, come back," Stacy said unhappily. She looked at Renée. "Is he right by doing that?"

"Mrs. David, I can't get involved. I'm only witnessing the signatures. However, off the record—if my husband and I separated, he'd do the same thing. I see Jonathan's point."

"Stacy, have you already arranged to move in with a man, or have a man move in with you?" I asked curiously.

"No."

"Then why argue over it? Finish reading the papers."

It wasn't long before she asked, "Why do you want me to change my last name back to my maiden name?"

"It's just a request. If I'm not mistaken, if it's in the papers, it can be done at no cost. If not, then there's a fee you have to pay. Why would you want to keep my last name?"

"You're going to give me the money today, right?" she asked.

"As soon as the papers are signed and notarized, you get your money. I included the clause about paying you early for December. I start payments of $125 in January."

We both signed four copies, and Renée began the process of notarizing them.

"Why four copies, Jonathan?" Stacy asked.

"One copy is for you and one for me. The other two are for our attorneys."

"Okay, is that it?" Renée asked.

"Yep." I wrote a check for $450, made payable to myself, and asked Renée to get a cashier's check made payable to Stacy.

"Why don't you just give me the cash?" Stacy asked, wide-eyed.

"Because I know how you are. I want receipts."

She wasn't happy about it, but Stacy cashed the check, took the money, and left the bank.

I took the papers straight to Mrs. Ingram's office and went back home.

It was finally over and done with, at least this part of it. But as they always say, *waiting is the hardest part.*

18

Are You Loving Life Right Now?

I'd successfully orchestrated getting the papers signed. I hated to resort to trickery to accomplish the feat, but with Stacy, I had to play her own game—and this time, I'd emerged the victor. The divorce would follow easily enough; the grunt work was done on my end. I handed the ball off to Mrs. Ingram, and it was her job to run the ball to the goal line—a piece of cake for her!

My next task at hand was Cynthia, who definitely was *not* going to be a cakewalk, but just the opposite; she would be a hard sell for sure. I called her that afternoon before going to work. "Guess what I did today?" I asked.

"I have no idea. There's no telling with you," she responded.

"I got the separation papers signed and hand-delivered them to my lawyer's office."

"Well, that's a good thing!" she said brightly.

"Yes, I think it calls for a celebration, don't you?"

I should have known I'd set myself up to have my bubble popped. Cynthia had no problem with cynicism, as I'd soon hear from her reply. "Just because you got the papers signed doesn't mean it's over, Jonathan. You still have, what, two months before the six months is up? Then you have another month or two for the judge to issue the divorce. A lot can happen in that amount of time, especially dealing with Stacy."

I sighed. "You sure know how to hurt a guy, don't you? I thought you'd have a more favorable response. I guess I haven't proven myself to you yet."

"No, not quite," she said, "but you're getting there."

"So I guess there's no cause for celebration in your eyes?"

"We'll see."

Cynthia and I spent Christmas together, and I admit I went overboard with gifts. I was trying desperately to win her affection. We had numerous talks about the subject. "Cynthia, I'm really developing strong feelings for you, and I don't know what to do with them," I said one afternoon.

"Well that's a good thing," she said. She seemed to like that phrase, as I'd hear it often.

"Tell me, *how* is it a good thing? I feel you have no feelings for me at all."

"That's not true," she said. "I let you stay overnight. That should tell you something."

"It does, but is the chemistry there between us? Do you have any romantic feelings for me?"

She looked a little uneasy. "Yes, I believe the chemistry *is* there, but it's going to take me a while to get over my last relationship, and I still have my doubts you'll get your divorce."

"What can I do to prove myself to you that I haven't already done?"

"Nothing. You're doing fine."

"I don't want to fall in love with you and not have my feelings returned. Mentally, I can't handle another failure," I admitted.

"Jonathan, just give it time, okay?"

We made plans for New Year's Eve. I was working the 8-4 shift and had taken New Year's Day off. We planned to go to a popular nightclub, but I warned Cynthia that Stacy might show up there, since it was her old stomping grounds. I just wanted her to be prepared.

As my luck would have it, we had a power failure at work that day, and I had to stay over to get the processes running again. I worked diligently to get everything back online, as I wanted to get out of there, and I kept in contact with Cynthia to let her know I was still trying. At 10:15 that night, I was finally allowed to leave. I called Cynthia from my cell phone to let her know I was on my way home to shower and change, and I'd be there as soon as possible if she was still interested in going.

"Yes, come on!" she said, much to my delight. Maybe this would be the turning point in our relationship; it was a new year, a new beginning to my life.

I arrived at her house around 11:15. When she opened the front door, I was completely in awe. It was the first time I'd ever seen her in a dress and heels, and I was simply overwhelmed. I followed her upstairs to her bedroom; she said she needed help with her shoes. She slipped the shoes on her feet and needed my help to fasten the straps. It was all I could do to hold myself back as I held her nylon-covered feet in my hands and fixed the straps.

We made it to the club with fifteen minutes to spare. We danced a few songs, brought in the New Year, then left at 1:00 to get a quick bite to eat at a Waffle House. I dropped a few subtle hints about a new beginning for the both of us, but I felt I wasn't making headway. As it turned out, I wasn't—we both just went to sleep that night.

We remained together throughout January and into February. Her birthday was the day before Valentine's Day, so I set my sights on that occasion before I broached the subject of intimacy again. "Cynthia, we've been seeing each other for five months now, and I'm beginning to wonder if there's even a spark on your end. You know how I feel, but I haven't the slightest clue as to your feelings."

"I'm getting there," she said, as always.

I kept telling myself she was waiting for my divorce to be finalized before we could take our relationship to the next level—but I was getting impatient. I know she got tired of me bringing the subject up.

I talked to a co-worker about the situation and he did have valid points; I was making myself too accessible. Every time Cynthia called, I was there. "Make yourself less available," he said, "and if she has feelings for you, she'll miss you." I'd never been a firm believer in the saying *Absence makes the heart grow fonder;* my thinking was that it only made the heart grow fonder if you *wanted* it to. If Cynthia didn't have the feelings I'd hoped, then I'd make her life easier by being around less.

The plan didn't work.

Shortly after Valentine's Day, I decided to go for broke and throw all my cards out on the table. "You know how I feel about you, right?" I asked her.

"Yes, of course I know. Why?"

"Because Stacy is out of my life now. I want a new beginning. I want romance and the intimacy that accompanies it. I want these things with you, but I just don't see it from you, Cynthia. I've been patiently waiting for over five months, and nothing has happened. If you don't feel the "spark" for me now, you never will."

I put my heart out on my sleeve, and wasn't expecting Cynthia's response at all.

"Jonathan," she said quietly, "if you feel you need intimacy right now, all I can say is that you'll need to go elsewhere to get it—because I'm just not ready."

Ouch! Her comment cut straight to the bone, and it hurt like hell! However, I'd set myself up; I knew there was a chance I'd get hurt in the process, but it was something I felt compelled to do for my own sake. I couldn't stay on the one-way street much longer. I took my friend's advice and made myself less accessible. I wasn't doing it to see if Cynthia would reveal her true feelings; instead, I was slowly beginning the process of detachment.

When I later talked to Cynthia and I did bring up the comment, she admitted it was the wrong thing to say. "It just came out wrong," she said. "I didn't intend for you to run away, but I understood you needed things I couldn't give you at that time."

"So was there a chance for us?" I asked. "I'm sorry; I just need to know."

"Yes, the chance was there. But you couldn't wait long enough for it to come to fruition."

Kimber came into my life soon afterwards. Kimber was apprehensive to meet me at first, because my divorce wasn't finalized, but she went against her own rules—and the rest isn't history, but the past, present and future.

I do remember Kimber and I making a bet about when my divorce would be final. The loser had to treat the winner to a romantic get-away for a night. I said the divorce would be final in April, and Kimber said it would be afterwards. Kimber won by a landslide: the divorce was finalized in June.

I was working the 8-4 shift. I'd just gotten home from work, and was lying on the bed when my phone rang. It was Mrs. Ingram's paralegal, Leigh. "Hey, Jonathan, how you doing?"

"I'm fine, just relaxing a few minutes. I had a rough day at work."

"Well, let me ask you a question—are you loving life right now?"

"Yes, I'd say so, why?"

"I got a phone call from one of my contacts at the court. You're now legally divorced, effective today!"

"That's great! Thanks so much for calling."

It's funny; as much as I'd looked forward to that moment, despite all the nights I'd laid awake thinking about how it would feel to be rid of Stacy, my reaction wasn't what I'd expected at all. In fact, I was sad. I told Kimber that day, and she sensed it in my voice, but she'd gotten to know me well enough by then and she understood. I didn't tell my parents until the next day. I wasn't in a celebratory mood, and I knew they *would* be.

I've seen people out celebrating and having a grand ole time when their divorce was final. Why didn't I feel this way?

Eventually, after a lot of thought, I realized that I already knew the answer. To me, divorce is a sign of failure; I'd failed again. When I married Stacy, I never envisioned it ending this way. I was abused every which way but loose. I'd worked myself into the ground. I didn't have a damn thing to show for the last twelve years of my life, because of Stacy and her kids; therefore, I'd somehow failed. I knew I'd done everything conceivably and humanly possible to make it work, but I wasn't able to work through all the issues.

My therapist and I talked about it at great length. "Your feelings are perfectly normal, Jonathan," Mr. Logan told me. "A lot of the hoopla you see on television is just that, a lot of hoopla. It's TV, so a lot of what you see isn't real. It's the writers' and producers' way of portraying life the way they *want* things to be. You've got a good woman with you now, and the rest of your life is ahead of you. Enjoy yourself, Jonathan. Don't look back. You can't change what's past."

*   *   *

I realized, while writing this, the point at which my memory went bye-bye. It was at the time I fell and broke my shoulder. Dr. Syriana said I was very fortunate that my Mother found me when she did, lying on the floor gasping for breath. Dr. Kashadi told me my "blackout" was my mind's way of telling my body to shut down to prevent self-destruction. That period of my life was the most difficult to write about, because I simply don't remember much of it. I can remember some things I did myself, such as going to physical therapy and watching Matlock on TV; but concerning Stacy, even though I may have known what was happening at the time, I have absolutely no memory of her existing during those fifteen months of my life. These memories may or may not ever surface. I had to rely heavily on my family to write about the events of that time.

Since my current condition surfaced, I've had every test I can think of that uses initials (EEG, EKG, MRI, etc . . .). The neuropsychiatrist who examined me for the bouts of double vision is the one who first noticed the evidence of the stroke on my MRI. Most of the doctors have concluded that the blackout fits a general profile as the most likely event to attribute it to.

19

Signs of Abuse: A Review

As I stated in my introduction, I'm not a psychiatrist, psychologist, or therapist; I'm just a layman who lived through twelve years of hellish abuse at the hands of a woman, a spouse in my case. In this chapter, I'll review what I feel were the seven major signs of domestic abuse in my life. I only wish I'd had the insight to see them earlier. I'm fully aware there may be many more that are not included in my list; therefore, my signs shouldn't be deemed as the latest scientific word, or as the only visible indicators. I strongly advise anyone in a similar situation to fully research the subject at both the library and online, and most importantly, to seek professional help with licensed doctors and therapists. Don't be ashamed to shed that "macho" image to get the help you need.

In the following section, I've included my own definitions for each sign. My definitions aren't clinical explanations but definitions that you, the reader, would more likely find useful. I've also included specific examples from the book, to illustrate how each sign was put into practice as an abusive tool in my life.

1. Control and Manipulation: The abuser needs to feel that they're in control at all times. Manipulation is just a tool to obtain the control they so desperately need. The abuser needs to feel responsible in making all decisions.

In my history with Stacy, one theme recurs repeatedly: control is usually a mask used to hide the abuser's own insecurities. Why did Stacy have these feelings of insecurity? She'd been popular in high school, as I learned from a coworker; she'd married her high school sweetheart immediately after graduation. It seemed she was the All American Girl with a bright, successful future.

Stacy's Dad unknowingly supplied the missing pieces of the puzzle during our many talks during the marriage, in which he repeatedly mentioned the temper tantrums she threw during her childhood to get her way. As a result, she'd been given everything she wanted. When she married her first husband, though, she found it wasn't so easy to have things her way. Her first husband wasn't as giving as her parents, and their marriage eventually ended badly in divorce; he refused to relinquish complete control to her.

I briefly mentioned Stacy's previous husband, her second, who had died of a massive heart attack in his thirties. To hear Stacy tell the story, he had a heart condition that wasn't discovered until after his death. To hear others talk, Stacy was the contributing factor to his death. Her games and manipulative tactics, along with her never-ending spending habits, had him so stressed that after a certain point, his body simply couldn't handle it anymore. I found a court transcript in the attic one day that I secretly read, and I now know some of the ordeals he endured—but for the sake of his family and to protect his integrity I've chosen not to reveal the details. I'd rather let him Rest in Peace.

During my first week of marriage, as I related, I felt as if I'd made a mistake; I told Stacy at that point I couldn't do it all by myself. But I allowed her to manipulate me early on in the relationship. A classic example occurred later that year, when she coerced me into calling the department store and requesting an increase on my credit card. I'd allowed her to control and manipulate me by using sex as bait.

2. Denial: First of all, the denial phase isn't intended to represent the person being abused; it's the *abuser* I'm referring to here. The abuser rarely has feelings of remorse for the actual violent act itself; they're more concerned with the fear they'll get caught by their actions. The abuse is always blamed on something else: their childhood, a bad day at work, the children misbehaving, or someone cutting in front of them in traffic. Any excuse can be valid in this stage, as an escape for the abuser to deny that *they* are the problem when they feel threatened.

For example: in my recollection of the night I met Stacy at the all-night restaurant, she became very upset with me, proceeded to take extra Xanax, and then threatened to run her car into a tree. There are two issues of denial in this scene.

First of all, she was sure I'd gone back inside the restaurant to call the police, and sped off with her son in the car. I followed her—but to avoid the possibility of getting caught for the medication abuse, she purposely led me to the police station, with the story I was trying to harm them. The attention was successfully transferred to me as the bad guy. I tried to tell the police of Stacy's actions that night, but my version was swept under the rug. Secondly, when her psychiatrist saw me the next morning in the mental institution, he immediately recognized the problem and had me released. When Stacy learned of this fact, she wasted no time contacting the insurance provider and switching doctors. She knew her doctor was on to her substance abuse, and her next medication visit might lead to her being detained.

Both of these incidents were successful, from her perspective; she escaped capture as an abuser.

3. Alienation of Family and Friends: Over time, the abuser will attempt to make you sever all ties with your family and friends. Again, this is based on insecurities. The abuser is scared that a family member or friend will be in contact with someone who may divulge information about him/her. The less contact with outsiders, the less chance of encountering someone who knows of his/her past or bad habits.

Stacy's first target in this respect was my son. My ex-wife had remarried, and I later found out her current husband had attended high school with Stacy—and he may have known something about her characteristics. She hadn't set her sights on my parents at that point; she was still trying to uphold the image she'd created of herself from the beginning. She had already been threatened once by the ex-boyfriend's Mother approaching my Mother with information.

However, Stacy was convinced she'd won them over for the time being. It wasn't until my parent's 40th anniversary party, which her ex-boyfriend's parents would be attending, that Stacy kicked things into overdrive. She was adamant that I wouldn't be attending; she didn't want me to be around the ex's parents for fear they'd talk about her. The method she used to accomplish her goal brings up the next sign: **Intimidation**.

4. Intimidation: This occurs when the abuser scares you into doing things their way. It can be accomplished simply with gestures, looks, and/or verbal orders. Destruction of property is often used with intimidation, to show the consequences of non-conformance to his/her demands.

In my situation, again referring to the 40th anniversary party, she told me that if I went against her orders and attended, I'd find my personal belongings packed in bags and sitting outside the front door upon my return. I consider myself blessed to have parents who are understanding and supportive. They were aware of the hell I was living through, and to keep the peace they put their own wishes and desires on the back burner. They'd long since known of Stacy's methods, and certainly didn't want to make things worse for me. Stacy's orders were intimidating to say the least, but also they fell into the next abusive topic: **Threats and Accusations**.

5. Threats and Accusations: This subject is very broad, and covers a wide variety of scenarios. It could be regarded as a form of control. *"If you do this I'll pack your bags,"* etc., as discussed in **Intimidation**. If the abuser notices a lack of attention towards him/her from you, his/her mind can easily misconstrue your activities as an escape plan, and so they have a need to retaliate. For a woman, it could be something as simple as noticing you looking at another woman. Most men do this at some point—it's in our nature—and most women recognize this as a traditional response. The abusive woman, however, will feel threatened.

Here's an example: my Mother was simply worried about my state of health after I started having panic attacks, and was calling more often than usual. Most of our conversations only required a simple yes or no answer on my part. Stacy misconstrued my end of the phone conversation in such as way as to believe that my Mom and I were plotting against her, and retaliated by going away for the weekend and having a brief affair; she was getting even with me for something she felt I had done, which in actuality was only in her mind. Once she'd realized the error in judgment she'd made, she admitted to the fact only because she was fearful her actions would give me an open invitation to divorce her for adultery, so she slowly began the next form of abuse: **Degradation of Self Esteem**.

6. Degradation of Self Esteem: The abuser starts making you feel unwanted, helpless, and (the most damaging) unattractive. The fear you'll walk away from the marriage is threatening to him/her.

In my case, Stacy began using simple comments, at first, about how lucky I was to have her. Comments such as: *"Everywhere I go I notice men looking at me; you should consider yourself lucky to be with me!"* After she'd convinced me how lucky I was, she changed faces: *"You're no good and nobody wants you,"* or *"You can't make it without me."* The most damaging to me was, *"My friends are always asking me what I see in you!"* The first two I could accept as just her opinion, but the last comment really got to me. Did her friends really say that? Do I look that bad? That was most damaging to my self esteem; I began to think of myself as undesirable. I can personally attest to the fact that if someone tells you something repeatedly over time, you'll begin to believe it. I was too wrapped up in myself at that point to realize that Stacy didn't really have any friends—and I shouldn't have worried about the opinions of the few women whom she could call acquaintances anyway.

7. Substance Abuse: The correlation between substance abuse and domestic violence seems to be strong, whether alcohol, street drugs or prescription medications are involved. In most cases, the substance abuse—or the lack of it to satisfy the body's cravings—leads to violent tendencies.

I deliberately saved this sign of abuse for last. I had very little, if any, knowledge of psychotic drugs before Stacy, and as a result of the way things played out, I have trouble imagining an abusive relationship without some form of substance abuse as a contributing factor. Stacy's downfall started with Xanax, known generically as Alprazolam. If taken as prescribed, it can be beneficial; however, if abused, the abuser's dependency on the drugs steadily increases. Xanax especially is highly addictive, and therefore very hard to break away from. According to my therapist, it's harder to break a Xanax addiction than it is to break a heroin addiction.

Stacy claims she was put on the medication when her previous husband died, but when I look back to the times we met and the frequency of her taking the little white, then orange, then blue pills, I firmly believe she'd been taking it longer than she'd admitted. The more she took, the more she needed to satisfy the urges her body craved; however, this is a common factor with any type of addiction. She'd also become addicted over the years to painkillers such as Hydrocodone, Vicodin, and Percocet. After the car accident, Stacy's addictions were too far advanced. Her violent tendencies had escalated to what my former therapist had feared: physical violence aimed towards me.

Her addictions to prescription medications overpowered her body and mind; as a result, she lost control of herself and her actions. Stacy was fully aware of the problem, but she wasn't willing to seek the help needed to save herself, much less our marriage.

Reflections

After everything I've learned about Stacy's childhood, and seeing firsthand her abusive tendencies escalate from bad to worse, I firmly believe that my marriage to her was simply lethal—doomed to fail from the very beginning.

So where did I lose control in our relationship? Well, as I said earlier, I never had it. How can you lose something you never had?

Everything happens for a reason; and had my life not unfolded the way it did, I wouldn't be where I am today. I married a wonderful woman in 2005, and she's been an unending source of support since my last marriage began to haunt me in earnest in late 2007. If not for Kimber, I would never have appreciated life as I do now; nor would I have experienced a marriage the way it's meant to be. She's simply a terrific woman.

I feel that someone, a Higher Power, was watching out for me during those 12 years of hell. I was able to work through most of it, and though I barely kept my head above water, I'm alive to tell about it. Now that I'm in a much better situation, all the physical damage caused by the stress and trauma of those years, including my ulcers and hernias, has been repaired.

Sure, there have been pitfalls. I'm still haunted by my past. I'm still unable to work. A simple privilege many people take for granted, driving an automobile, has been taken from me until my problem can be diagnosed and treated. I have to depend on my family to take me to doctor, psychiatrist, and therapy appointments. My psychiatrist has come to the conclusion that I may have Post Traumatic Stress Disorder; but it's treatable.

One of my co-workers once told me, "The things that don't kill you only make you stronger." I can now thoroughly appreciate his advice.

My body may be showing signs of the past, and my mental abilities may be slightly damaged, but I survived. I went to hell, and came back to tell my story.

I see my life differently now; every day is a new experience to enjoy. I'm very thankful to have my family, who never left my side throughout this whole traumatic ordeal. But most of all, I'm grateful that I still have the one precious thing that can never be replaced: my life, and the bright future that lies ahead of me—something I never thought I'd ever see again.